Canadian Mini Books:
Famous People

Grades 2-4

Written by Ruth Solski and Sharon Mather
Illustrated by Tom Goldsmith and Ric Ward

About the authors:

Ruth Solski has been an educator for over 30 years and is the founder of S&S Learning Materials. As a writer she strives to provide teachers with useful tools to bring the joy of learning to children.

Sharon Mather is a French immersion teacher for the Lambton Kent District School Board. She has studied French in France and Spanish in Spain, and taught ESL in Japan for three years. This is her third teacher resource book in social studies.

ISBN 978-1-55035-885-8
Copyright 2008
All Rights Reserved * Printed in Canada

Published in Canada by:
S&S Learning Materials
15 Dairy Avenue
Napanee, Ontario
K7R 1M4
www.sslearning.com

At A Glance

Learning Expectations	Leif Eriksson	Jacques Cartier	Samuel de Champlain	James Wolfe	Louis-Josph de Montcalm	Joseph Brant	Laura Secord	Harriet Tubman	Sir John A. Macdonald	Nellie McClung	Mini Book Activites
Listening Skills											
• Follow oral directions to produce a mini book	•	•	•	•	•	•	•	•	•	•	
• Gain historical information through listening	•	•	•	•	•	•	•	•	•	•	
Reading Skills											
• Develop oral fluency in a group or with a partner	•	•	•	•	•	•	•	•	•	•	
• Recall information and details on a topic	•	•	•	•	•	•	•	•	•	•	
• Make predictions in a story	•	•	•	•	•	•	•	•	•	•	
• Connect text of story to other situations	•	•	•	•	•	•	•	•	•	•	
• Develop independent reading	•	•	•	•	•	•	•	•	•	•	
Language Skills											
• Retell the historical story orally	•	•	•	•	•	•	•	•	•	•	
• Sequence historical events in order	•	•	•	•	•	•	•	•	•	•	
• Use vocabulary to review previously learned skills	•	•	•	•	•	•	•	•	•	•	
• Compare and contrast historical characters on a chart or Venn diagram	•	•	•	•	•	•	•	•	•	•	
Social Studies Skills											
• Recall information taught											•
• Identify historical figures visually											•
• Identify historical figures through reading											•
• Identify importance of historic figure											
• Complete historical sentences											•
• Create historical puzzles and games											•
• Research other historical figures											•

Table of Contents

Teacher Assessment Rubric

Student's Name:_____

Criteria	Level 1	Level 2	Level 3	Level 4	Level
Understanding Concepts	Little	Some	Often	Frequently	
• Demonstrated understanding of the basic concept of famous Canadians					
• Visual identification and recognition of famous Canadians and their importance					
Communication Skills					
• Use of correct vocabulary relating to historical figures and their feats					
• Ability to read information books with confidence and understand their contents					
• Participation in group discussions and readings					
Language and Creative Skills					
• Ability to recall and express historical events and information orally					
• Ability to recall and write historical events and information					
Social Studies Skills					
• Ability to recall and use learned information to solve problems during game situations					
• Demonstrated understanding of the importance of historical figures in the development of Canada					

Comments:_____
_____
_____

Student Self-Assessment Rubric

Name:_____

Put a check mark in the box that best describes your performance. Then, add your points to determine your total score.

Expectations	My Performance				
	Needs Improvement (1 points)	Sometimes (2 points)	Often (3 points)	Frequently (4 points)	My Points
✓ I listened well to oral instructions.					
✓ I produced a neat, attractive mini book.					
✓ I participated well during all oral reading sessions.					
✓ I understodd and could read the written text used.					
✓ I was able to talk about and describe what learned about Famous Canadians.					
✓ I was able to use the information learned to complete other historical activities.					

Total Points: _____

Which famous Canadian did you find the most interesting?_____

_____

Are there any other Canadian heroes that you would like to learn about?

_____

_____

Why is it important to learn about people who have made important

contributions to Canada?_____

_____

Introduction

Canadian Mini Books: Famous People provides ten reproducible reading booklets pertaining to famous figures that played an important role in Canada's history and development.

Students benefit from this approach in several ways. Their involvement in developing the reading material provides added motivation to enjoy and appreciate the content. In addition, the manipulation of the booklets provides added interaction with the text. Interaction is further enhanced in two ways. Each page of every booklet has a statement that tells the story of the historical character. Some statements are illustrated and some are not, allowing students the opportunity to visually interpret text and assist in the creation of the story. Some of the booklets have illustrated pages for which students must select from a bank of statements and cut and paste the most appropriate words to accompany the images. These booklets are recommended for students with the strongest reading skills. Students will gain practise in reading the booklet at school or at home.

Organization

There are four different styles of booklets. The style of booklet used for each is indicated in the **Table of Contents**. Full instructions to make each booklet are to be found immediately after this introduction.

Timelines of the ten characters are to be found at the front of the book as well. These may be enlarged and used on a bulletin board or on a clothesline-like string and held on with clothes pegs or paperclips somewhere in the classroom. The timeline will assist students to organize and put events in order. The figures may also be reproduced and used by the students to develop individual timelines. The figures may be coloured, cut out, and glued onto a long strip of paper in order of their birth or dates of their accomplishments.

The bulk of the book is organized by historical figure. Each section includes one to two pages of information on the figure. These information pages can be used as teacher information, read together as a whole group exercise, or assigned to individuals. Note that the reading level for these information pages is between grades three and six, so care must be taken to match reading level with student ability. the mini booklets themselves are designed for grades two to four.

The final pages of the book contain a series of activities designed for further use with the mini books to encourage interaction with the finished product, to draw out specific reading comprehension and social studies skills, and to serve as assessment opportunities.

Suggestions for Use as **Classroom Reading:**

1. Do a picture walk of the book before reading it.
2. Read in small groups.
3. Have booklets at a centre for independent work while the teacher is working with small groups for reading or writing.
4. Have students work on oral fluency and then read to an elbow partner.
5. Do a group read of the same booklet with one person reading aloud and the rest of the students whispering.
6. Have students read aloud one on one to a reading buddy.
7. Have students answer questions from a generic question list on the board: who? what? when? where? why? how?
8. Stop at a key point and have students make predictions.
9. Have students make connections to the text: text to self, text to world, and text to text connections.
10. Have students retell of the story in their own words.
11. After reading the story, put the booklet away and as a group rewrite on chart paper the main events.
12. Use booklets as a follow up to viewing the video clips called *History by the Minute* available at www.histori.ca. Videos about Jacques Cartier, Samuel de Champlain, Vikings, Underground railway, Nellie McClung, and Laura Secord are all available.

Additional Suggestions for Follow-Up Activities:

1. Have the students each create one different question about the text.
2. Decide in a group if the person is a hero or not; brainstorm what makes a hero.
3. Look at words in the text and make lists of parts of speech: nouns, verbs, adjectives, adverbs, etc.
4. Look at the words in the text and find synonyms, antonyms, and homonyms.
5. Look for words that rhyme with...
6. Use words in the text to make crossword puzzles or word searches.
7. Fill in a comparison chart using five Canadian heroes with headings like: lifespan, contributions, challenges, rewards, etc.
8. Do a Venn diagram on chart paper to compare and contrast two Canadian historical figures.
9. Create a graphic organizer using the information in one or several booklets.
10. Create a game of Jeopardy using one hero for each heading and giving points for different questions (with answers found in the info booklets) worth 10, 20, 30, 40, and 50 points.
11. Write a letter to one of the Canadian heroes using a correct letter format. Ask them three questions and make connections with their life to your own life, to another text or story, or to the world.
12. In small groups, act out in a short drama that happened in the booklet.
13. Find out three more interesting facts about a Canadian person and display it in an interesting fashion (poster, booklet, newsletter, journal entry, poem, bookmark, book jacket, as a biography, trifold pamphlet, etc.).
14. Create a game board using questions based on the lives of the heroes you have studied.

Leif Eriksson
970-1020

Jacques Cartier
1491-1557

Samuel
de Champlain
1570-1635

James Wolfe
1727-1759

Louis-Joseph
de Montcalm
1712-1759

Joseph Brant
1742-1807

Laura Secord
1775-1868

Sir John A.
Macdonald
1712-1759

Harriet Tubman
1820-1913

Nellie McClung
1873-1951

Instructions for Making Accordion Booklets

> LOUIS-JOSEPH de MONTCALM, page 36
>
> LAURA SECORD, page 55
>
> HARRIET TUBMAN, page 65

1. For each booklet, photocopy all full pages of the templates, one copy per student. For Harriet Tubman also photocopy the sentence strips (page 71).

2. Have the students colour and draw the necessary pictures. For Harriet Tubman, have the students cut out sentence strips and glue on the appropriate pages.

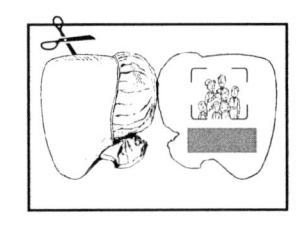

3. Cut out the drawings' outer edges, being careful to not cut apart the two flip images on the same page (Montcalm's accordion booklet has only one form per page).

4. Tape along the right side of the page at the furthest edge of the drawing to the furthest left side of the next page's drawing so the page numbers of the books are in order from left to right.

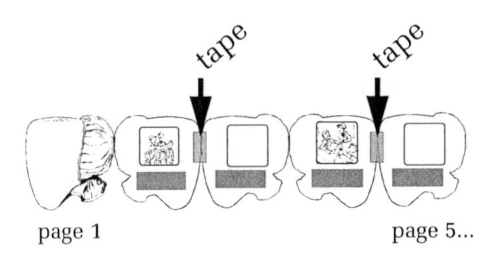

5. Fold the booklet like an accordion (or a fan) so that only the cover is seen and the other pages fan under, hidden from sight until the page is turned.

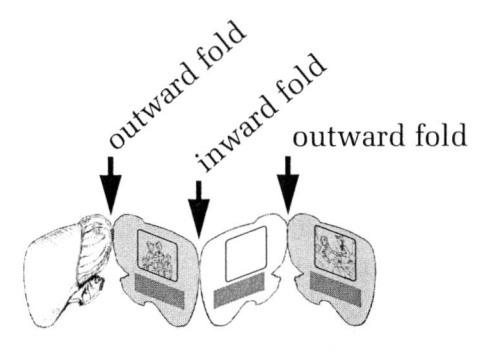

finished booklet

Instructions for Making Mini Booklets

LEIF ERIKSSON, page 16

SIR JOHN A. MACDONALD, page 62

NELLIE McCLUNG, page 74

1. Cut out the template pages.

2. Photocopy the two pages of the mini booklet onto 11x17 or 11x14 paper if photocopied at 90% original size. The two pages can also be photocopied and glued onto 11x17 paper instead. Put mini page 1 beside mini page 2 and mini page 5 beside mini page 6.

3. Have the students draw the missing pictures and colour the pictures provided. For Nellie McClung, have the students cut out sentence strips and glue on appropriate pages.

4. Trim the outside. Fold this big paper in half lengthwise.

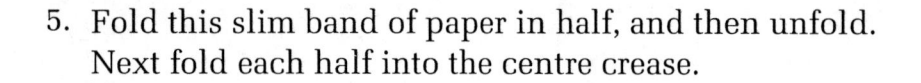

5. Fold this slim band of paper in half, and then unfold. Next fold each half into the centre crease.

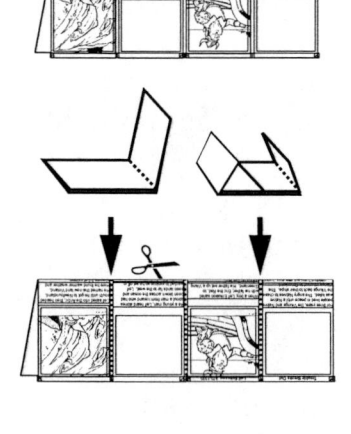

6. Undo the folds. You now have four mini pages separated by creases. With scissors make a slit at the fold at the top of the middle two pages.

7. Take the two outer pages and push them together.

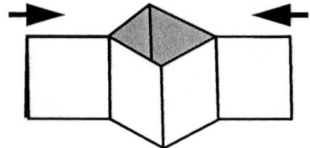

8. Fold all the pages to the right to form a book. Flip the cover page to the front of the book.

Finished booklet

Instructions for Making Card Booklets

> JACQUES CARTIER, page 19
>
> JAMES WOLFE, page 30

1. Photocopy the templates. One copy of each per student, by making double-sided copies as follows: photocopy pages 1 and 8 back to back with pages 2 and 7; then photocopy 3 and 6 back to back with pages 4 and 5. The templates could also be photocopied singly and then glued back to back in the same way as the instructions indicated for photocopying. For James Wolfe, also photocopy the sentence strips.

back to back   back to back

2. Have the students draw the necessary pictures and colour the ones provided. For James Wolfe, have the students glue the sentence strips under the appropriate pictures.

3. Place pages 2 and 7 face up on the desk and place pages 4 and 5 on top facing up.

place 4&5 on top ➤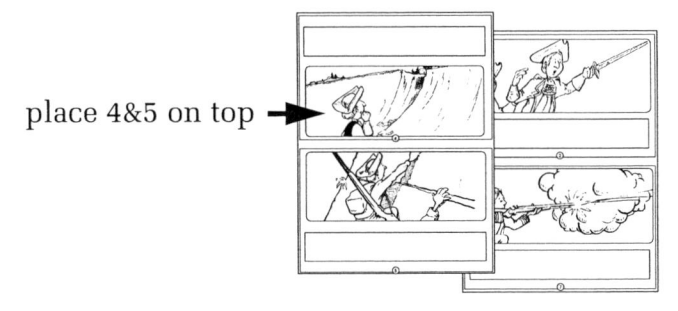

4. Fold the two pages neatly down the centre. Staple the spine. Turn the booklet so page 1 is facing up.

staple ➤ 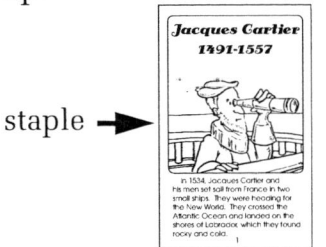   staple ↘

Instructions for Making Shape Booklets

SAMUEL DE CHAMPLAIN, page 25

1. Photocopy pages.

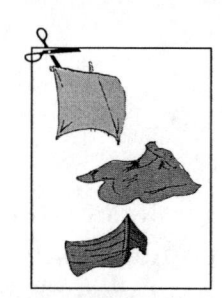

2. Colour and cut out each of the seven shape templates (i.e. the boat, the forest, the cloud, etc.)

Glue tab

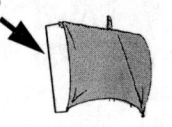

3. Using the picture on page 25 as a guide, glue each shape template using the glue tab to cover the text boxes on the booklet base page (page 26).

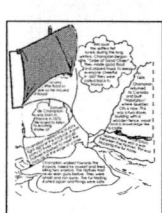

JOSEPH BRANT, page 44

1. Photocopy the templates and the sentence strips.

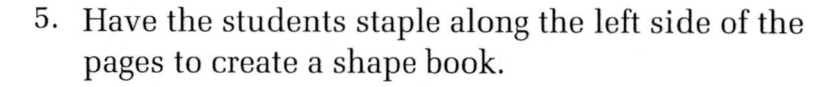

2. Cut out each sheet. (Have students cut out if they are of sufficient dexterity.)

3. Have the students cut and paste the sentence strips onto the correct page.

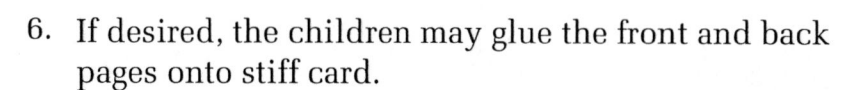

4. Have the students colour the pages.

5. Have the students staple along the left side of the pages to create a shape book.

Staple

6. If desired, the children may glue the front and back pages onto stiff card.

Leif Eriksson
(970 – 1020)

Leif Eriksson was a Viking. The Vikings were a fierce group of people from Northern Europe. They loved to travel and explore new lands with their ships. They would often attack and steal from villages on the way. The Vikings discovered North America 500 years before Christopher Columbus.

Leif's father was a famous explorer named Eric the Red. Leif grew up wanting to explore new lands, too. Around the year 1000, Leif bought a ship from a man named Bjarni. Bjarni was a trader from Iceland. His ship was once blown away in a storm and he had seen lands far to the west.

Leif repaired Bjarni's ship and set off in search of the unknown land. Days later he and his crew sighted land. They went to shore and found giant glaciers and a huge slab of rock. This might have been Baffin Island.

Leif sailed further south. After a time he came to a land where the weather was warm and nature was plentiful. They had reached North America. No one is sure where the Vikings first landed. It may have been the coast of Newfoundland, Nova Scotia, or New England. The rich new land was everything Leif had hoped for. He named it Vinland the Good.

After Leif returned home, other Vikings set out to explore the new land. Leif's brother Thorvald was one of them. He led a trip the next year but it was not a success. Thorvald and his men met Native men and fought with them. During the fight, an arrow hit Thorvald. Before he died he told his men that they had found a good land but they would not be able to settle in it. His men buried him and went home.

Thorfinn Karlsefni was another Viking who went to Vinland. He and his wife decided to try and settle there. They set out with a large number of ships carrying 250 men and women. The first winter was very hard. The settlers grew hungry and sick and they fought each other. In time, they too met the Native people. They called them Skraelings and fought with them. They no longer felt safe in the new land and decided to return to Europe.

④ **Winter in Vinland**

Leif and his men decided to stay in Vinland for the winter. They built huts of earth and wood and ate berries that looked like grapes. The next spring they sailed home with a ship full of wood.

⑤ **Leif's Brother Arrives**

The next year, Leif's brother, Thorvald Eiriksson, sailed to Vinland. He found Native people sleeping under kayaks. The Vikings and the Natives fought and eight Natives were killed. One person escaped.

③ **Searching for Land**

Leif sailed into the Arctic, then headed south until he got to Newfoundland. He named this new land Vinland. Here he found warmer weather and streams full of salmon.

② **Dreams of Adventure**

As a young man, Leif heard stories about a man from Iceland who had been blown across the ocean and seen lands far to the west. Leif wanted to explore so he set off in search of this far land.

⑥ **Vikings, Go Home!**

This Native returned with more men in kayaks who fought against Thorvald and his men. An arrow hit Thorvald and killed him. His men buried him and went back to Greenland.

Viking Settlers ⑦

A year later, Thorfinn Karlesfni and his wife arrived in Vinland with 250 settlers. The first winter the Vikings were hungry and sick, but they also celebrated the birth of Thorfinn's son, Snorri. This was the first European born in North America.

① **Leif Eriksson 970-1020**

When a boy, Leif Eriksson sailed with his father, Eric the Red, to Greenland. His father set up a Viking colony on this land.

Trouble Breaks Out ⑧

For three years, the Vikings and Native people lived in peace until a Native was killed. The angry Natives chased the Vikings back to their ships. The Vikings returned to Greenland.

Jacques Cartier
(1491 – 1557)

Early in 1534, two small ships set sail from France. An experienced sea captain named Jacques Cartier was the leader. Cartier's name would become one of the best known in Canadian history.

On this famous voyage, Cartier passed through the Strait of Belle Isle near Newfoundland and Labrador. He sailed past the rocky shores to Gaspé Peninsula. Cartier landed and erected a cross to claim the land for France. An Iroquois chief, Donnacona, became angry at Cartier's actions. Cartier did not like this and took the chief and his sons. Later he let Donnacona go, but he took his two sons back with him to France.

Cartier returned to the New World with Donnacona's sons a year later. They showed Cartier a great river, which he named the St. Lawrence River. The river took Cartier to an Iroquois village called Stadacona. It was nestled at the foot of a great rock, where Quebec City now stands. Donnacona greeted Cartier warmly. He was glad to have his sons back.

Cartier sailed on to a Native island village called Hochelaga. This island would one day become Montreal. Cartier stood on top of a steep mountain on the island and saw rapids up the river. He knew that he could sail no further up the river. He returned to Stadacona where he spent a very cold winter. Many of his men fell sick with scurvy, a disease caused by a lack of fresh fruit and vegetables. The Iroquois showed Cartier how to cure scurvy with the bark and needles of cedar trees. In the spring, Cartier and his men were glad to set sail again for France.

Five years later, Cartier returned to Canada once more to help colonists build a settlement. Cartier's men spent a lot of time collecting what they thought were valuable gems. After a year, Cartier left the settlement without permission and returned home with the precious cargo.

Cartier's "treasure" turned out to be worthless stones. The king was not happy with him and never sent him to sea again. Today Cartier is still admired for his skill in exploring the St. Lawrence, the key to the North American continent.

Jacques Cartier 1491-1557

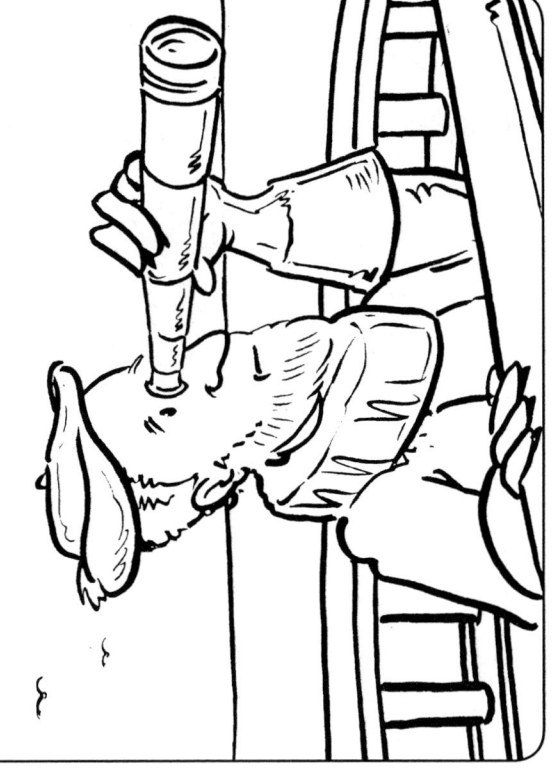

In 1534, Jacques Cartier and his men set sail from France in two small ships. They were heading for the New World. They crossed the Atlantic Ocean and landed on the shores of Labrador, which they found rocky and cold.

1

When Cartier returned five years later, the Iroquois were no longer friendly. They were angry their chiefs had died in France. Cartier waited for a year for more settlers. When they finally came, Cartier returned to France.

8

7

In the spring, Cartier's men loaded all the furs that the Native people had traded onto his ships. Before he sailed he invited Donnacona and other Iroquois chiefs on board. They were taken prisoner and taken to France.

Jacques Cartier sailed around the Gulf of St. Lawrence and stopped at the Gaspé Peninsula where he found the Native people friendly at first. Cartier and his men put up a large cross claiming the land for the King of France.

2

3

When Donnacona, the Iroquois chief, argued with Cartier about putting up the cross, Cartier captured Donnacona and his sons. Donnacona was let go but Cartier took his two sons back to France with him on the ship.

Cartier returned to Stadacona for the winter. Many of his men fell sick and died. Many were cured when the Iroquois showed them how to drink a tea that had vitamins in it made from the bark of the cedar tree.

6

5

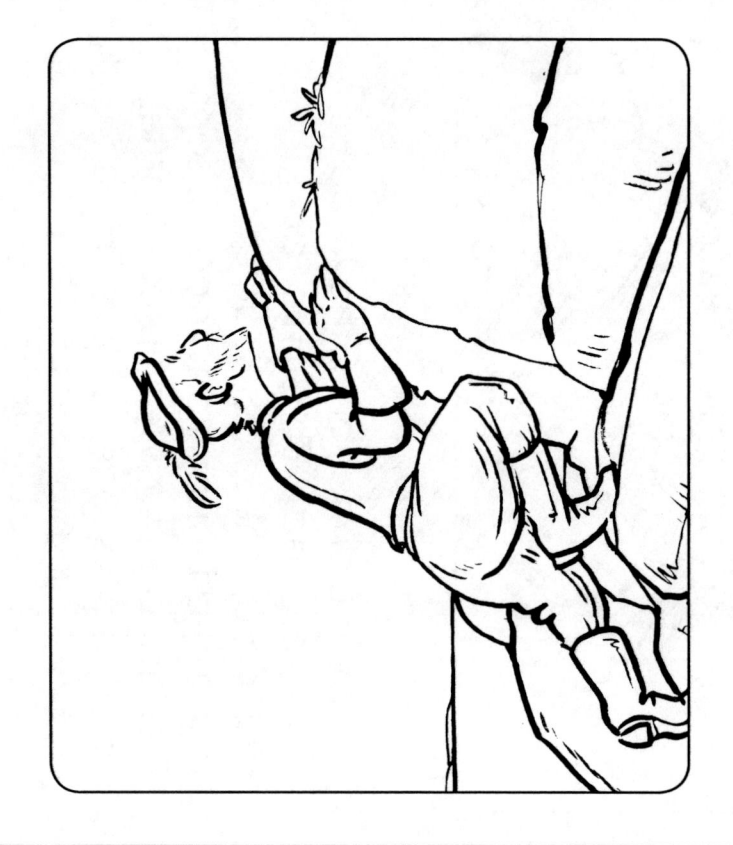

Cartier sailed further up the river to a Native village on a large island called Hochelaga where he climbed a steep mountain. He named this mountain Mount Royal, or Montreal. He could see rapids on the river and knew he could not sail further up.

In 1535, Cartier set sail for the New World again. He returned Donnacona's sons. They showed Cartier a great river that led to a freshwater sea. The river led Cartier to a native village called Stadacona where Donnacona greeted him warmly.

4

Samuel de Champlain
(1570 – 1635)

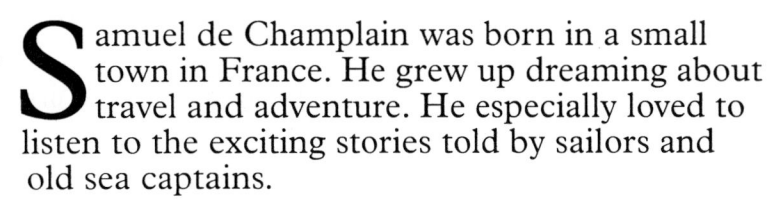

Samuel de Champlain was born in a small town in France. He grew up dreaming about travel and adventure. He especially loved to listen to the exciting stories told by sailors and old sea captains.

In 1604, French leaders decided to build a permanent settlement in the New World. Champlain begged to go along. He had a natural skill in drawing maps, which made him very useful on the trip. Soon he knew more about the Atlantic coast than anyone.

Champlain's first winter in Acadia was long and cold. It was hard to store enough food and supplies. Many of the settlers lacked fruit and vegetables and became ill with scurvy. Champlain, however, was a good-natured, happy man even when times were hard. He started the "Order of Good Cheer" to keep up the settlers' spirits. Each night a different member would plan a menu and prepare a feast. There would be songs or a play for entertainment. The Order helped keep everyone's mind off winter.

In 1607, leaders in France told Champlain and the settlers to come home. They were unhappy that the fur trade was growing so slowly. Champlain was disappointed but he knew he had proven that he was an expert explorer.

Champlain wanted to succeed where others had failed and create a New France. He persuaded the King of France to start a colony at Quebec. Champlain believed that Quebec could be the gateway for a successful fur trade. He knew there was great fur-trading territory along Canada's many lakes and rivers. Champlain also believed that the rivers of Quebec would lead him far into unexplored land. He hoped the rivers would take him to the Western ocean and the riches of China.

Champlain landed at Quebec in 1608 and began to build the "Habitation". This was a large two storey building surrounded by a high wooden fence and a moat. It had a large entrance gate and a drawbridge like a castle. When the Habitation was finished, Champlain proudly raised the fleur-de-lys flag of France. He believed the tiny fort would be the beginning of a great colony.

Champlain began to explore Canada. He travelled with a gun because there was a great war going on between the Native tribes. The Huron, Algonquin, and Montagnais tribes who lived north of the St. Lawrence River were fighting a war

Samuel de Champlain

against the Iroquois nations to the south. Each side wanted to control the fur trade. The war made it unsafe for peaceful traders to travel with their furs.

Champlain decided to help the tribes living north of the river defeat the Iroquois. He joined a Huron war party travelling south. They moved cautiously. No fires were lit and they moved at night. Finally they reached a long, narrow body of water that is now called Lake Champlain. There they met a group of Iroquois. The two groups decided to fight the next day at dawn.

At daybreak, the Iroquois warriors began to advance. Wearing light armour and carrying a musket, Champlain walked towards the enemy army. The Iroquois had never seen anything like it. They fired arrows at him but Champlain kept walking. He aimed and fired his gun with a shocking roar that echoed across the lake. Two of the Iroquois chiefs fell, their wooden armour pierced by musket balls. A second musket fired and a third Iroquois chief dropped. The Iroquois warriors had never fought against men with guns. They ran away afraid.

Champlain had won a great victory. Now the traders could travel safely along the rivers. The Habitation grew busy as Natives exchanged furs for axes, blankets, food, and other items.

Champlain was finally free to do what he loved best. He could explore unknown places and discover new things. He would see the great rivers and lakes that he had heard the Native people talk about. Champlain spent several summers exploring and mapping nearby areas.

In 1615, Champlain started on the longest of his voyages. He was going to Huronia, the land of the Huron nation. For many days Champlain and his group paddled their canoes across lakes and rivers. They carried their canoes past waterfalls and rapids and slept under the trees at night. Finally they reached Lake Huron.

The Hurons led Champlain to their land. The Huron nation was a powerful one. They lived in groups of longhouses protected by high, wooden fences. They were farmers who grew corn, beans, and squash.

Champlain lived with the Hurons for nearly a year and learned about their customs. In the spring he returned to the Habitation at Quebec. Although he never discovered the Western ocean or the route to China, his voyages truly put Canada on the map, and is now known as the Father of New France.

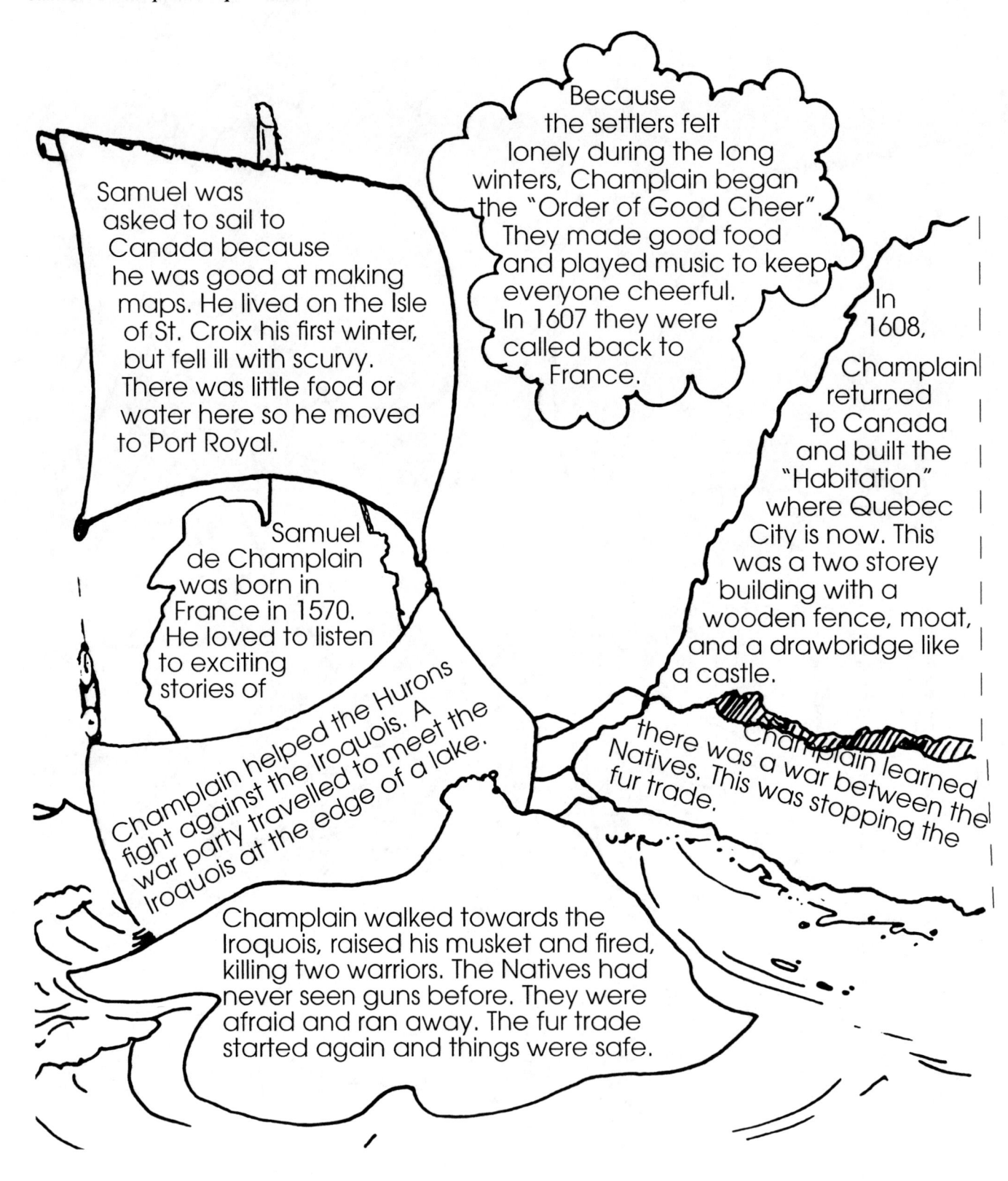

Samuel was asked to sail to Canada because he was good at making maps. He lived on the Isle of St. Croix his first winter, but fell ill with scurvy. There was little food or water here so he moved to Port Royal.

Because the settlers felt lonely during the long winters, Champlain began the "Order of Good Cheer". They made good food and played music to keep everyone cheerful. In 1607 they were called back to France.

In 1608, Champlain returned to Canada and built the "Habitation" where Quebec City is now. This was a two storey building with a wooden fence, moat, and a drawbridge like a castle.

Samuel de Champlain was born in France in 1570. He loved to listen to exciting stories of

Champlain helped the Hurons fight against the Iroquois. A war party travelled to meet the Iroquois at the edge of a lake.

Champlain learned there was a war between the Natives. This was stopping the fur trade.

Champlain walked towards the Iroquois, raised his musket and fired, killing two warriors. The Natives had never seen guns before. They were afraid and ran away. The fur trade started again and things were safe.

Student Instructions

1. Colour the shapes.

2. Cut out these shape templates.

3. Glue the shapes onto page 26 to cover up the text.

4. Flip up the shapes in order to read the story.

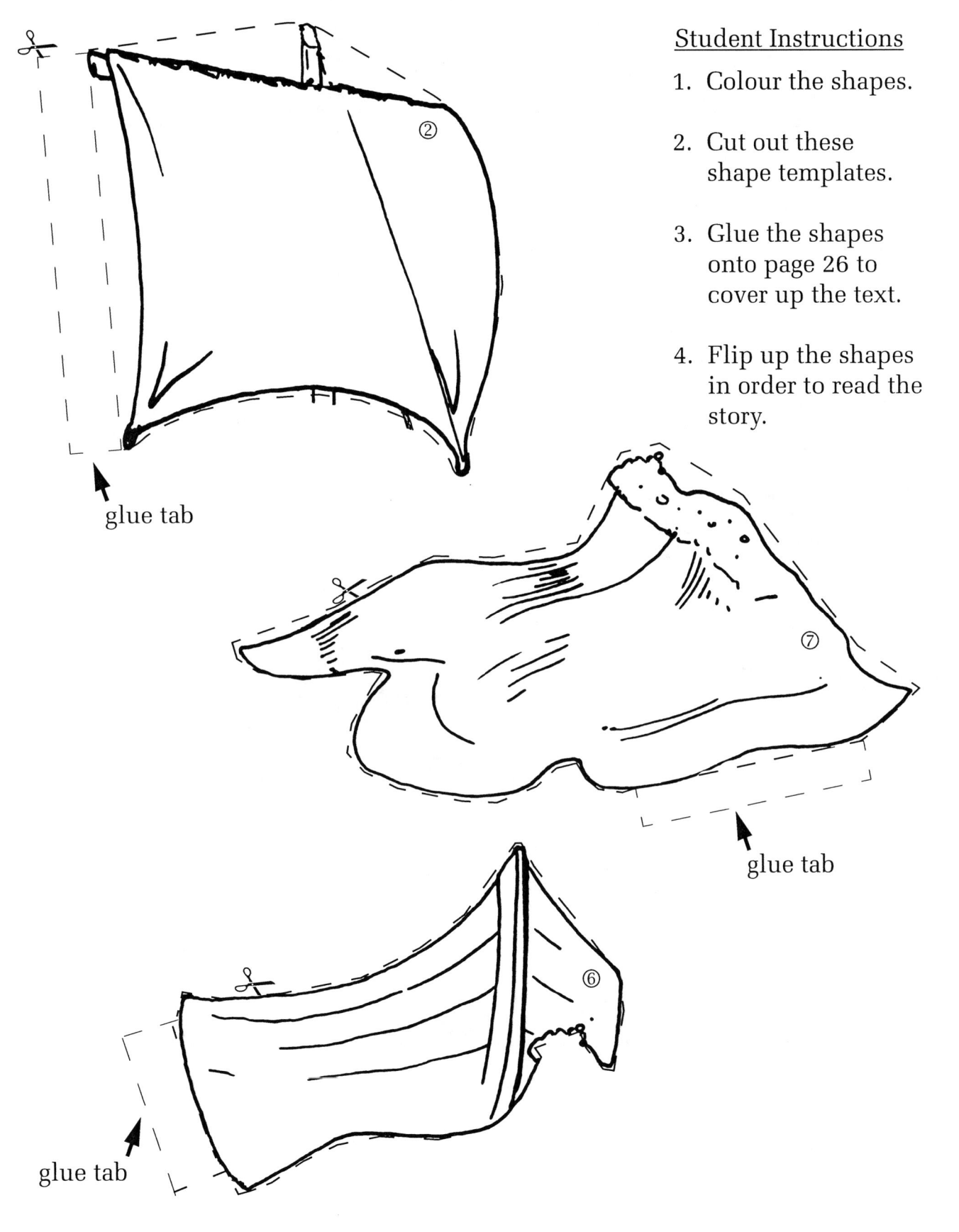

glue tab

glue tab

glue tab

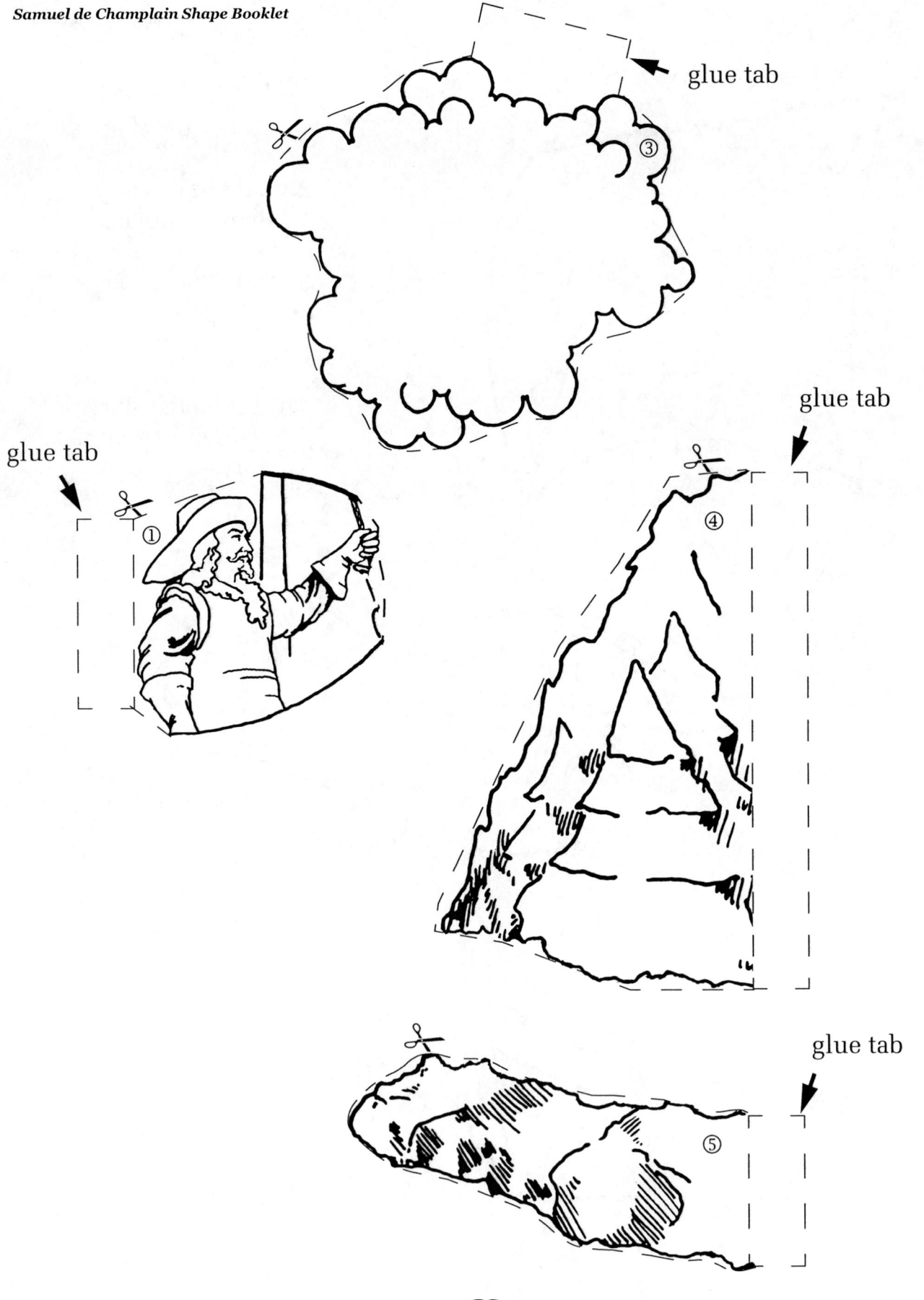

glue tab

glue tab

glue tab

glue tab

James Wolfe
(1727 – 1759)

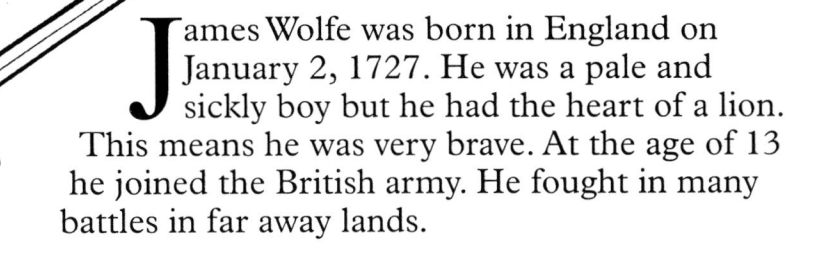

James Wolfe was born in England on January 2, 1727. He was a pale and sickly boy but he had the heart of a lion. This means he was very brave. At the age of 13 he joined the British army. He fought in many battles in far away lands.

In 1758, James was made a general. He was sent to Canada to help fight the French. After a great victory in Nova Scotia, General Wolfe and his army sailed up the St. Lawrence River to Quebec. Wolfe fired his cannons at the town for three months but his attacks were in vain. The town was surrounded by stone walls and sat high on a cliff. As long as the French stayed inside they could not be beaten.

With winter coming fast, Wolfe decided to try and draw the French into the open. He found a dry stream bed two miles away that wound up the face of the cliff. On the night of September 12, 1759, Wolfe and his men slipped away quietly. Under the cover of darkness four thousand men scaled the cliff climbing two by two.

The next morning, the French were shocked to see thousands of British red coats suddenly standing just outside the city walls. The French General, Louis Joseph de Montcalm, quickly brought his own army forward to meet them on the Plains of Abraham. Wolfe waited until the French troops were just 20 metres away and then ordered his men to fire. The roar of the muskets was deafening and the air was thick with white smoke. When the air cleared, the French army was in confusion. Many frightened soldiers were running away while hundreds of others lay injured or dead.

Wolfe led his men forward and chased after the fleeing army. His bright red uniform made him an easy target. He was shot in the wrist but continued to lead his men. He was shot twice more during the fight. He fell to the ground wounded so badly that he could not recover. His men gently carried him off the field out of the line of fire. Wolfe died without knowing of his victory over the French.

(8)

James Wolfe
1727-1759

(1)

30

6

3

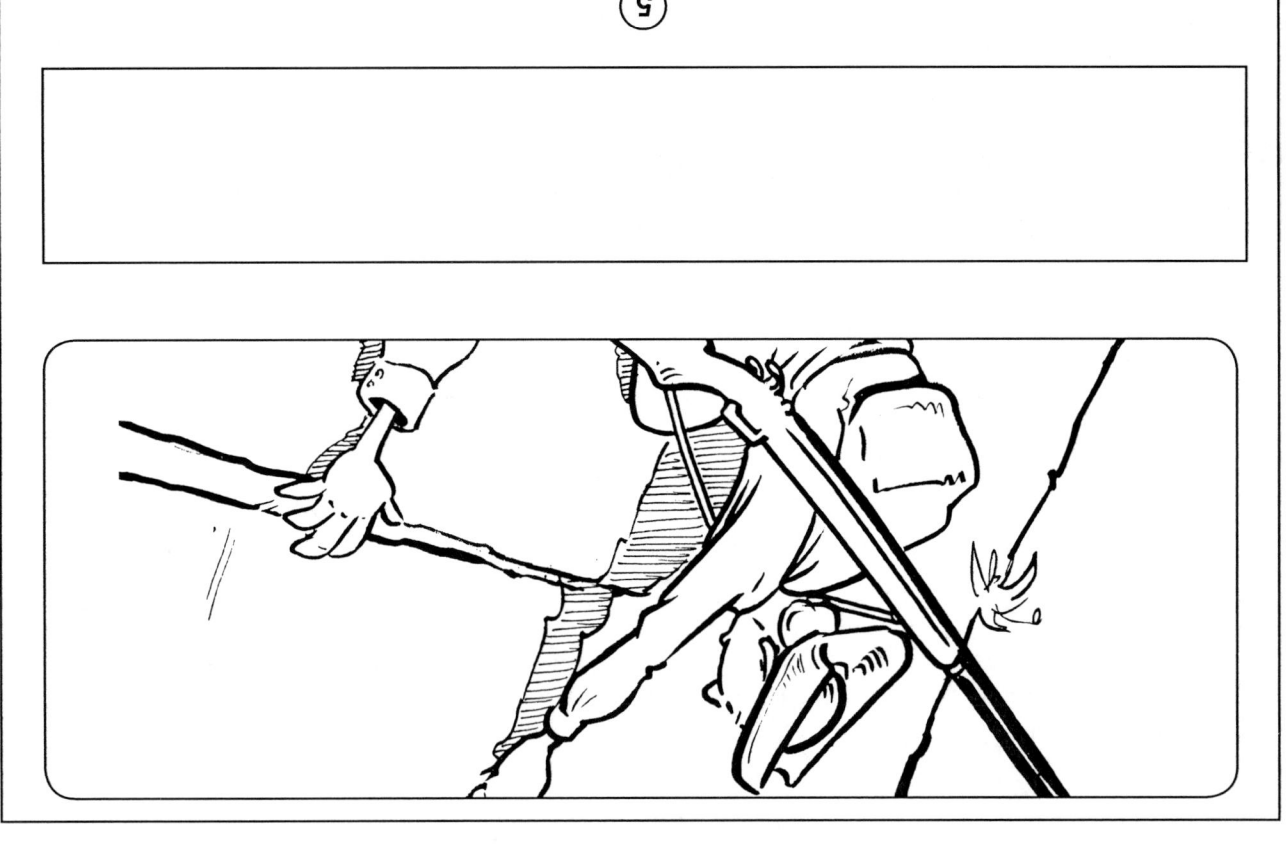

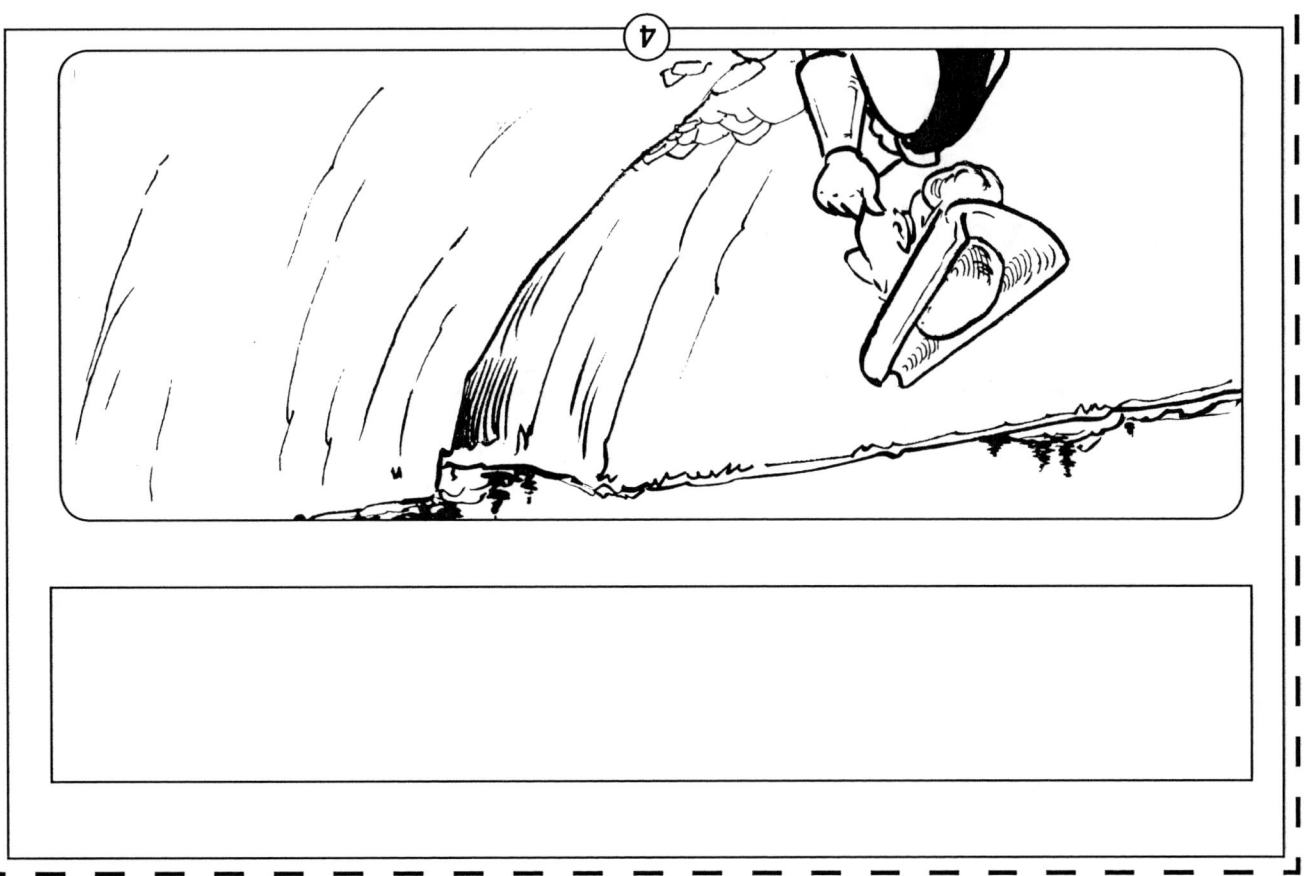

Wolfe, who was dressed in red and leading his men, was an easy target. He was shot in the wrist, and then later in the stomach and the chest. His men carried him off the field. He died before learning of his victory. (8)

James Wolfe was born in England in 1727. He was a sickly boy but was very brave. His father was an army officer. At age 13, James joined the army, too. By the time he was 18 he had fought many battles. (1)

In 1758, Wolfe was sent by the British to fight the French in Fort Louisburg in Nova Scotia. He won the battle. In June 1759, Wolfe sailed up the St. Lawrence to Quebec with more than 9,000 men. (2)

Wolfe ordered his men to wait until the French were only 40 metres away, then to kneel and fire. The roar of thousands of muskets was deafening. The air was filled with smoke. The French army was left confused, injured, or dead. (7)

In the morning, General Montcalm saw thousands of British red coats standing in line on the Plains of Abraham above Quebec City. He was shocked! He brought his own army forward to meet them. (6)

For three months, Wolfe shot his cannons at Quebec City and at General Montcalm's French soldiers. He knew his attacks were useless because Quebec was surrounded by stone walls on top of a high cliff. (3)

In September, Wolfe looked for a better way. He found a dry stream bed two miles upriver that went up the cliff. The path was so rugged that the French thought it impossible for the British to get up. They did not guard it. (4)

On September 12th, 1759, Wolfe's men made a noisy attack to distract the French while Wolfe and his ships slipped away quietly. At 4:00 in the morning, 4,000 of Wolfe's men climbed up the path on the cliff, two by two. (5)

Louis-Joseph de Montcalm
(1712 – 1759)

Louis-Joseph de Montcalm was born in 1712 in France. He reluctantly joined the army when he was nine years old. He would have much preferred a quiet life but his family expected him to become a soldier. Over the years he fought in many wars and was wounded five times.

In 1756, Montcalm agreed to lead the French army in North America. He was very successful in his military career but he was unhappy living in the colony. It was rough and he wanted to be back home in southern France with his family.

When General Wolfe and his men lay siege to the town of Quebec in 1759, Montcalm defended it well. After several months Wolfe's men found a secret way to scale the cliffs. They appeared suddenly one morning on the Plains of Abraham just outside of town.

If Montcalm had stayed behind the walls surrounding Quebec the battle may have ended very differently. Other French troops could have arrived to help fight Wolfe from behind. Instead of waiting, however, Montcalm chose to attack the British.

Montcalm mounted his black horse, raised his sword, and led his army into battle. Many of his men were untrained settlers and not prepared for the fight. When the French were a short distance from Wolfe's lines of troops, the British suddenly fired their guns at the French. Montcalm watched many of his men fall and his lines collapse. Others ran away in fear. Montcalm could not control them.

In all of the confusion, Montcalm was shot in the stomach and the leg. His men helped him to stay on his horse while he painfully and proudly rode back to the town. Montcalm died the next morning at dawn. He was buried in the Ursuline Convent in Quebec far from his home in France that he loved so much.

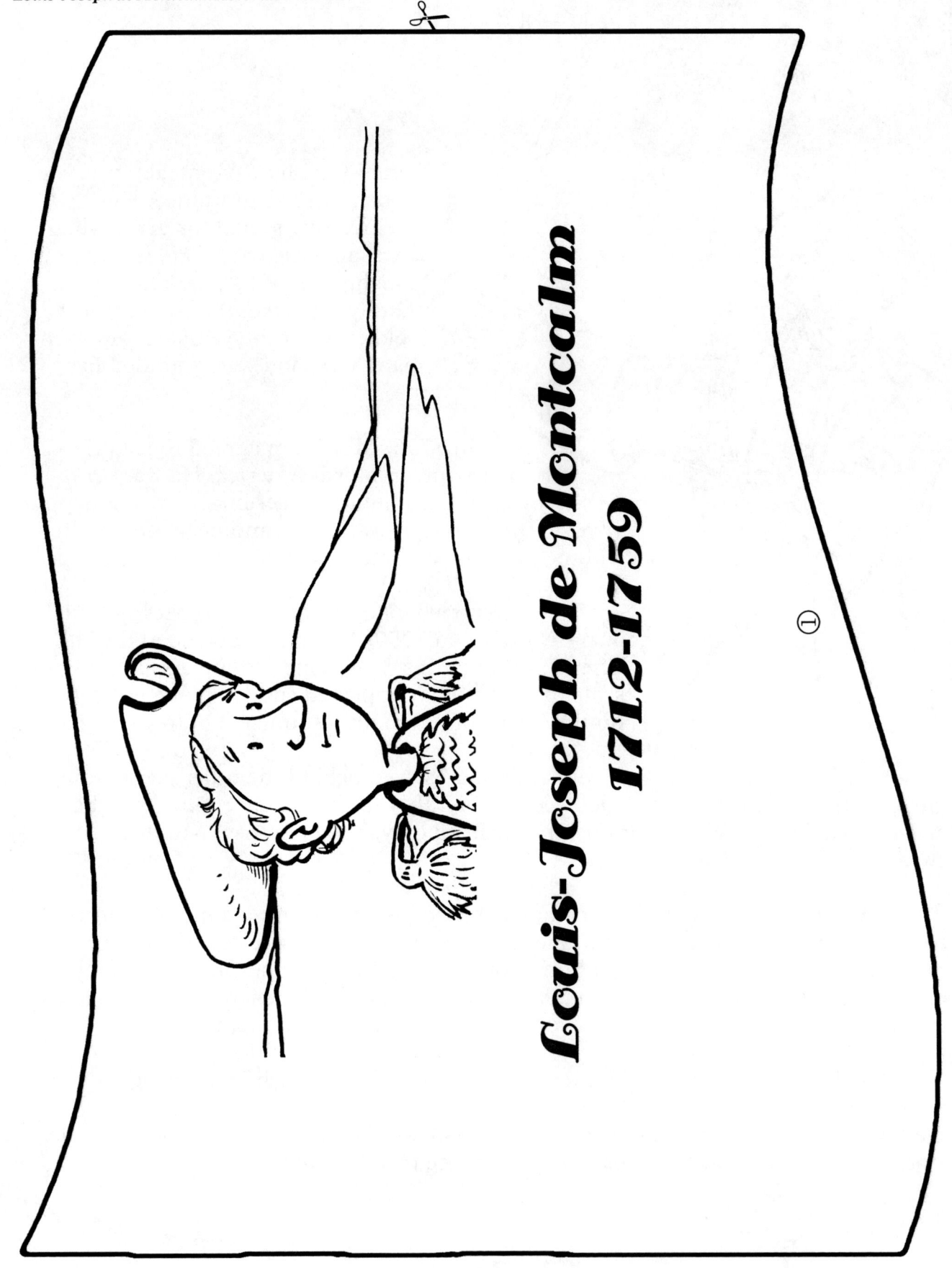

Louis-Joseph de Montcalm 1712-1759

①

Louis-Joseph de Montcalm was born in France in 1712. He wanted to live quietly but his family wanted him to become a soldier. He joined the army at the age of nine. He fought in many wars and was wounded five times.

②

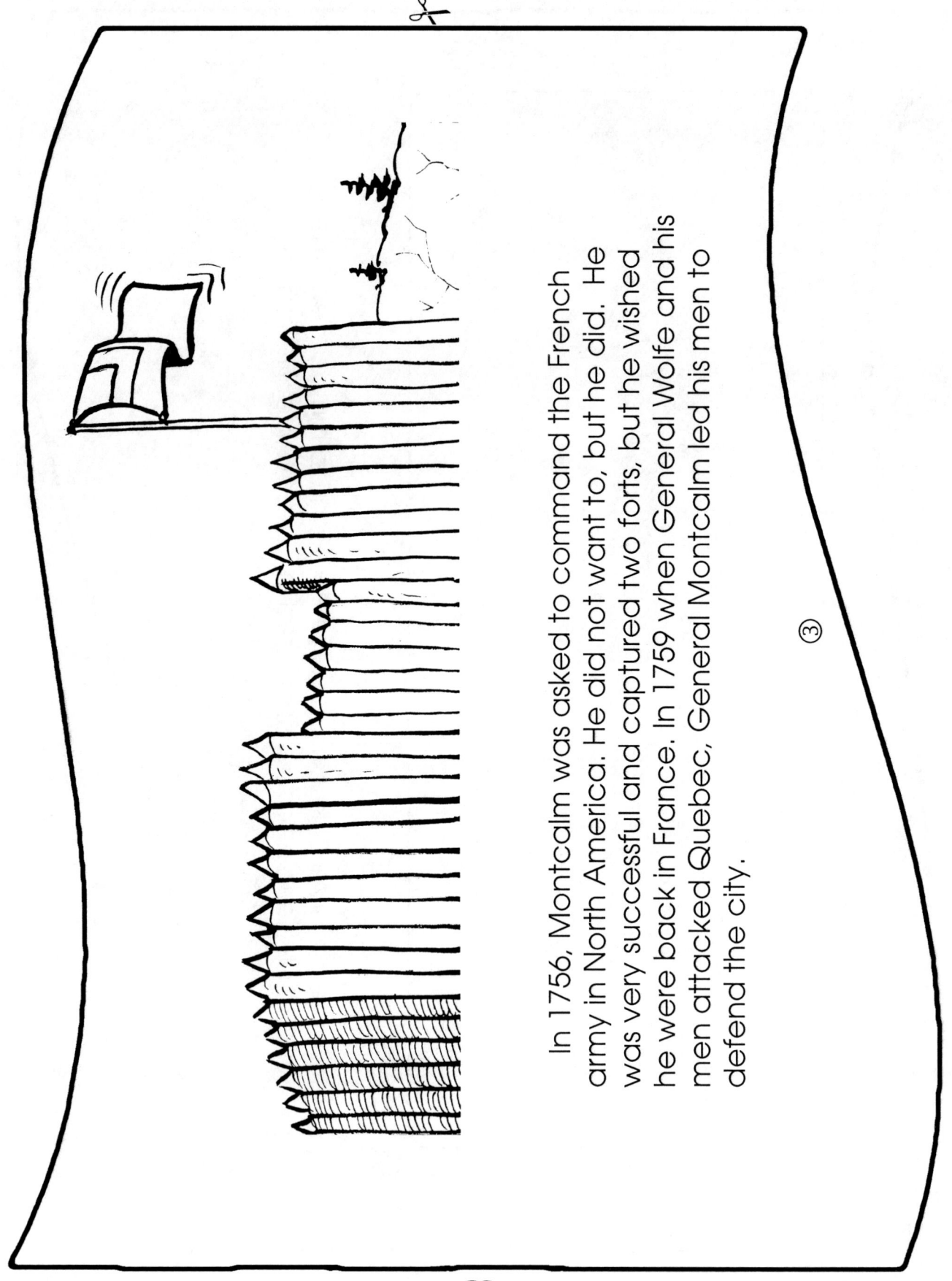

In 1756, Montcalm was asked to command the French army in North America. He did not want to, but he did. He was very successful and captured two forts, but he wished he were back in France. In 1759 when General Wolfe and his men attacked Quebec, General Montcalm led his men to defend the city.

③

If Montcalm had stayed behind the walls surrounding Quebec he might not have lost the battle. Help from other French troops could have arrived to fight Wolfe. Instead of waiting, Montcalm chose to attack the British.

④

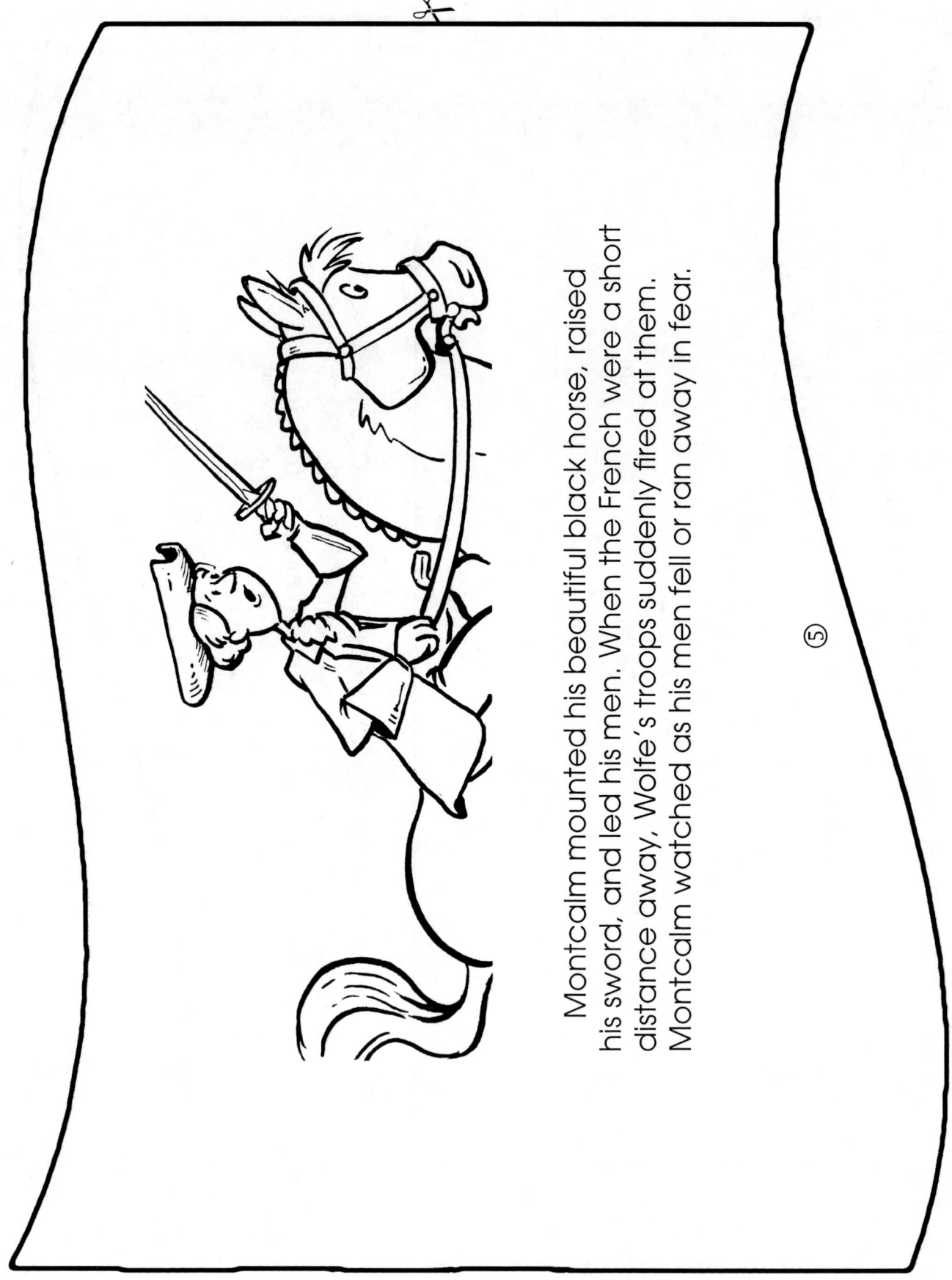

Montcalm mounted his beautiful black horse, raised his sword, and led his men. When the French were a short distance away, Wolfe's troops suddenly fired at them. Montcalm watched as his men fell or ran away in fear.

⑤

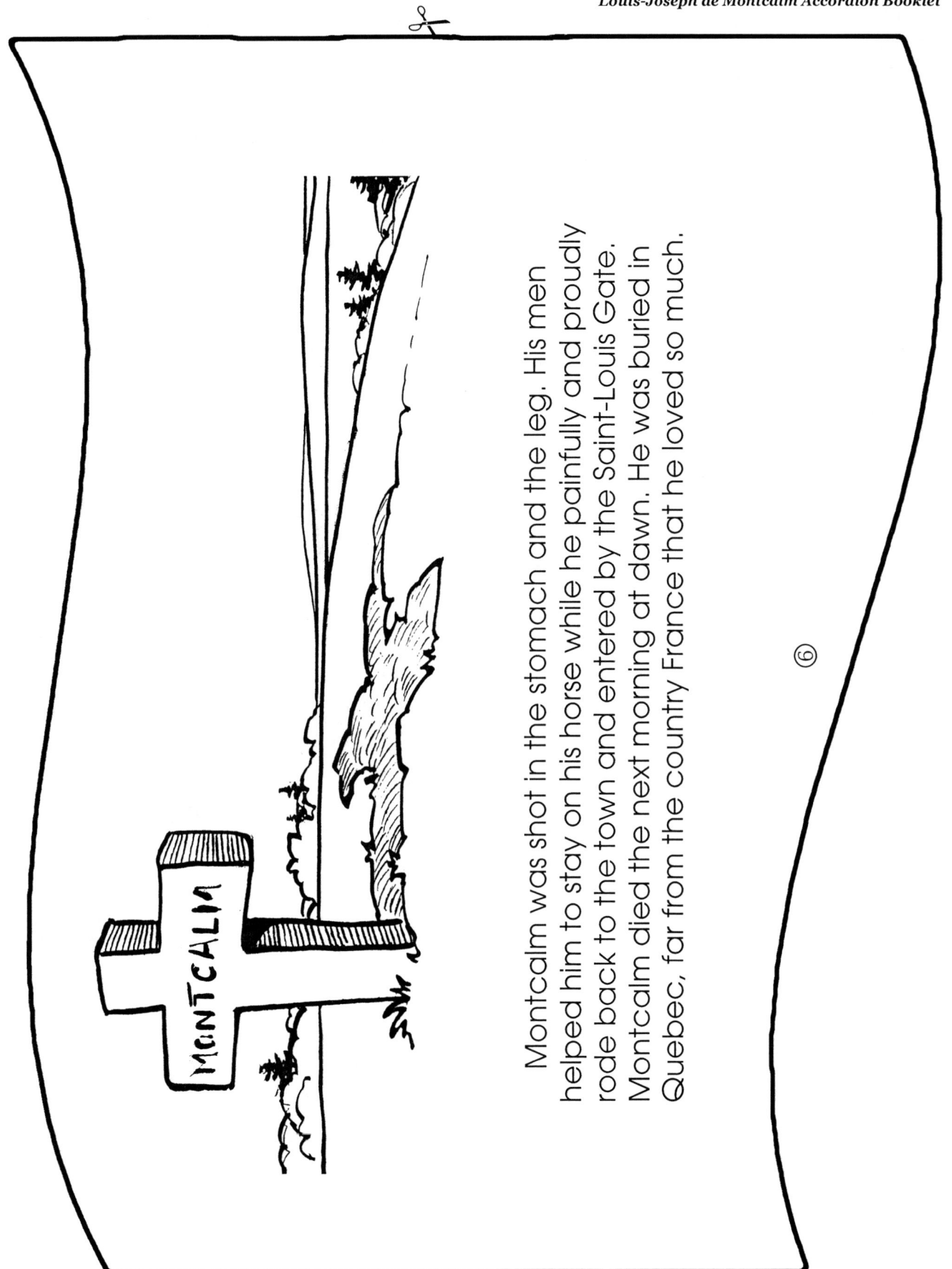

Montcalm was shot in the stomach and the leg. His men helped him to stay on his horse while he painfully and proudly rode back to the town and entered by the Saint-Louis Gate. Montcalm died the next morning at dawn. He was buried in Quebec, far from the country France that he loved so much.

⑥

Joseph Brant – Thayendenegea
(1742 – 1807)

Joseph Brant was a Mohawk. He was born in 1742 on the banks of the Ohio River. His parents named him "Thayendenegea" which means "strength".

Joseph attended a British school where he learned to speak English. He also studied western history and literature. Eventually he helped an Anglican missionary communicate with his people. He translated a prayer book and some of the Bible into Mohawk.

Joseph left school to serve under Sir William Johnson. Sir William was the British superintendent of the northern Native people of America. He was very popular with the Natives and was especially close to the Mohawk tribe. In 1759, he married Joseph's sister Molly in a traditional Mohawk wedding ceremony.

Joseph served under Sir William during the French and Native War of 1754 to 1763. At the age of 13 he followed Sir William into battle, along with other braves from the school. After the war, he worked as an interpreter for Sir William.

In 1768, Joseph married Christine, the daughter of an Oneida chief. They had two wedding ceremonies, one Native and one Anglican. The couple lived on a farm and had two children. In 1771 Christine died. Two years later, Brant married Christine's sister Susannah. Susannah also died of the same disease a few months after the wedding.

In 1775, Joseph was sent to England to find out if the King would help the Iroquois keep their land if they supported the British in the American War of Independence. He met with the King twice and a special dinner was held in his honour. The King agreed to give the Iroquois land in Canada if they supported the British. Joseph decided the Iroquois should help the British.

Joseph Brant – Thayendenegea

During the war some Native tribes sided with the Americans while others fought for the British under Mohawk Chief Brant. In 1778, Brant and his warriors destroyed the town of German Flatts in New York. The Americans then destroyed two Native villages. Brant and his men set out to destroy the town and fort at Cherry Valley. The soldiers stationed at the fort were not prepared for the attack. Many people were killed and houses were burned. The fort was abandoned and the event was called the "Cherry Valley Massacre".

Brant and his army brought fear and destruction to many areas but his forces were eventually defeated. In 1779, an army of 3,700 American patriots destroyed Iroquois fields, orchards, and granaries. The destruction greatly discouraged the Iroquois.

After the war, Brant helped secure peace treaties between the Americans and the Native tribes. He tried but could not get a fair land settlement for his people.

In 1784, the governor awarded Brant a grant of land on the Grand River in Ontario. He led 1,843 Iroquois Loyalists from New York State to this site. The group was made up of Mohawks, Cayuga, Delaware, Nanticoke, Tutelco, Creek, and Cherokee. They settled in small tribal villages along the river.

When Brant discovered that they did not own the reservation, he travelled to England to protest. The British government refused to grant the Natives ownership of the reservation, but paid them money for the land they had lost in the American War.

The Natives used the money to build a sawmill, a gristmill, and a school on the reservation. The Mohawks also built an Anglican church called "Her Majesty's Chapel". This simple wooden structure survives today as the oldest Protestant church in Ontario.

Brant was awarded many ornaments for his military service. He also received a pension and a large area of land at the Head of the Lake, which is now Burlington. Brant fought for the rights of his people for the rest of his life. He built a large house of cedar logs and lived there with his third wife, Catherine.

He, Joseph Brant, died at his home on August 24, 1807, and. He was buried at Her Majesty's Chapel on the reservation. The city of Brantford, Ontario, is named after him. A replica of his original home now stands on the same site. It was opened in 1942 as the Joseph Brant Museum.

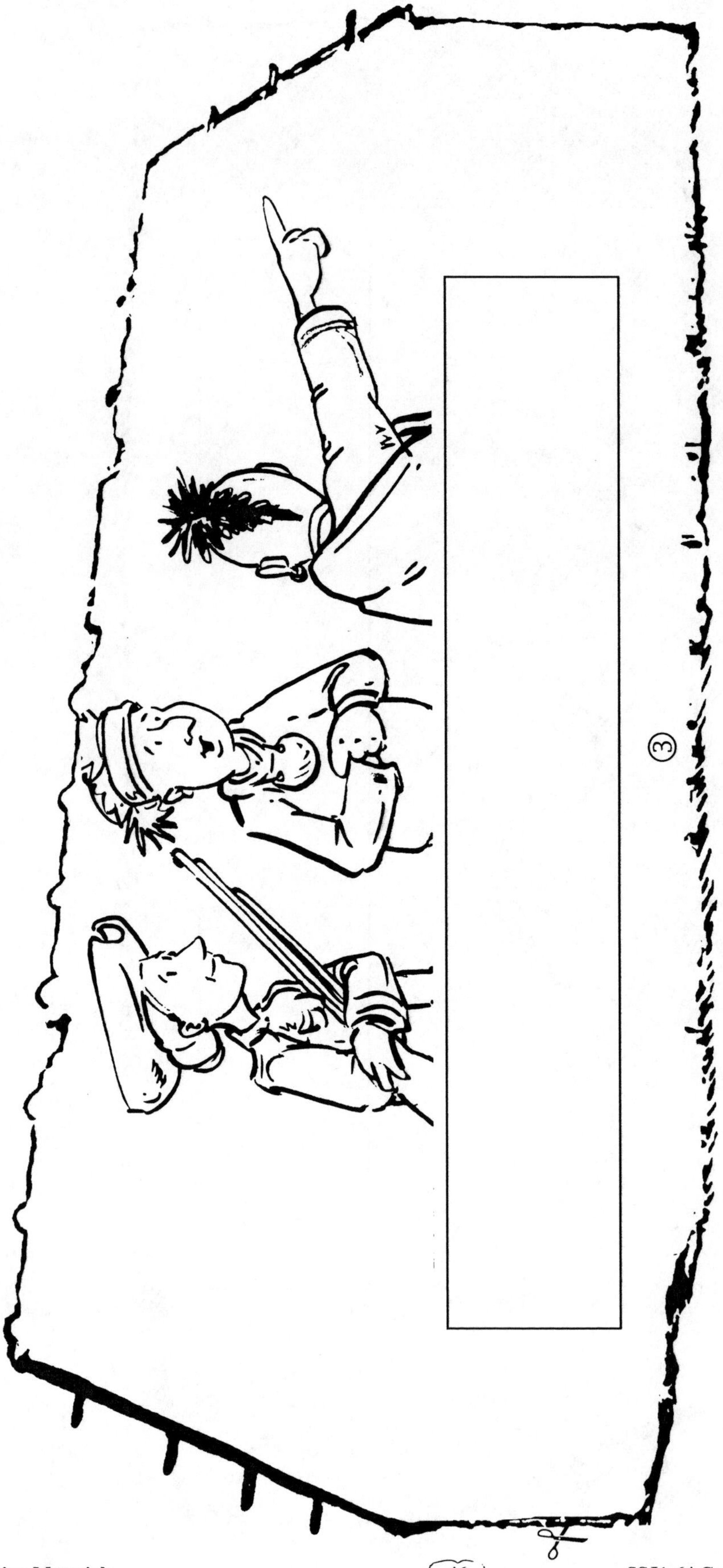
3

⑤

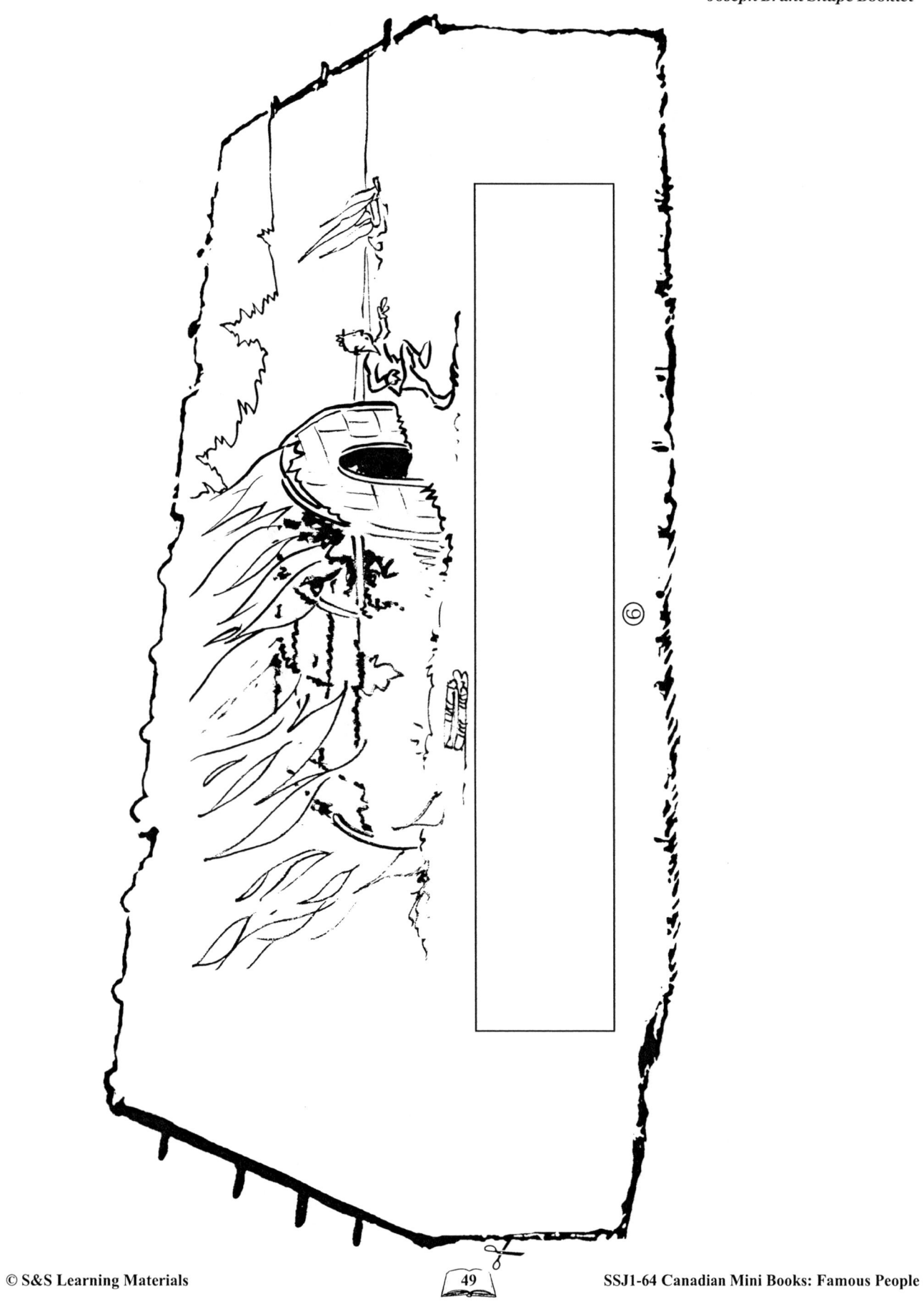

⑥

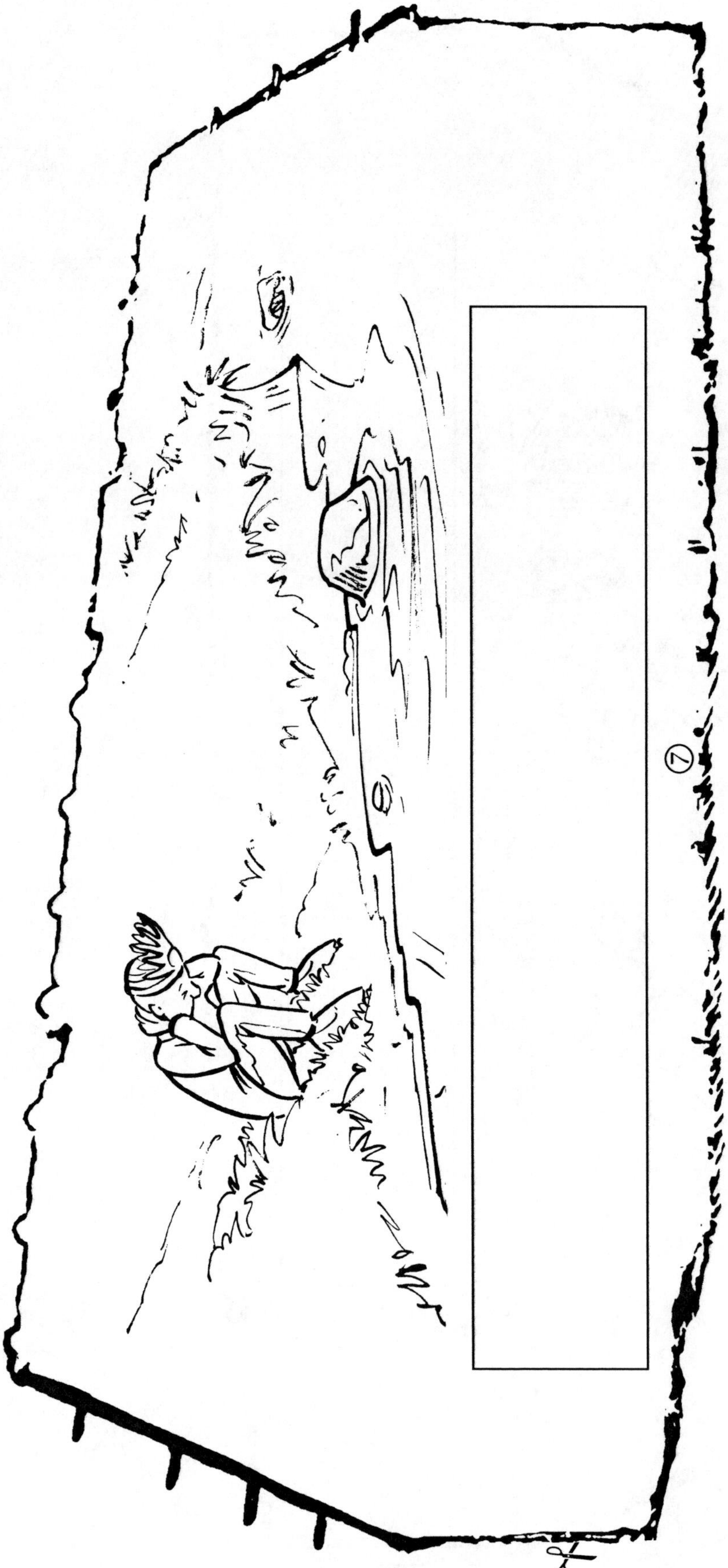
7

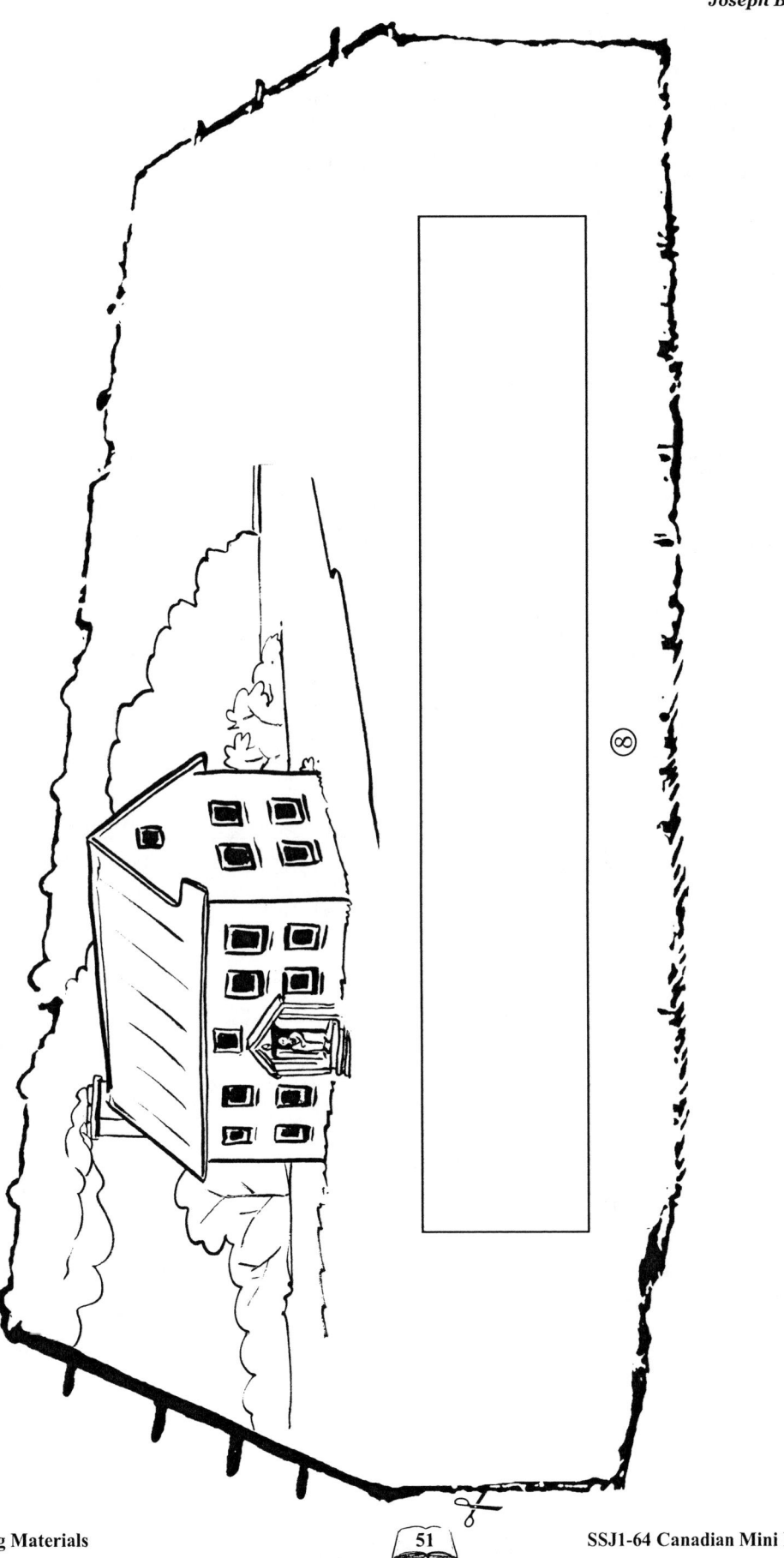

⑧

Sentence strips for Joseph Brant:

In 1742, Joseph Brant was born to a Mohawk Chief who gave him the Iroquois name "Thayendenegea" meaning "strength." He went to a British school where he learned to speak English well.
                                                                    p. 2

When he was 13, Joseph worked for Sir William Johnson, a British soldier sent to care for Natives. Joseph helped Sir William's soldiers fight the French during the Seven Years' War and then helped him communicate with Native peoples.   p.3

When the Americans wanted to break free from Britain, the British asked Joseph for help. Because he wanted his land to be safe, he sailed to England. The British said they would give Joseph's people land, so he decided to help the English.   p. 4

Joseph travelled through Iroquois land telling the tribes that they should help the British save their land. When the leaders of the tribes agreed they made Joseph "War Chief of the Six Iroquois Nations".   p. 5

Joseph led the Iroquois against the Americans but he did not want women or children hurt. The Iroquois lost their land, homes, and fields and were forced to flee for safety to British forts.
                                                                    p. 6

When the war was over, Joseph was angry because the British gave the Iroquois land to the United States. In 1784, Brant and his people were given a place to live on both sides of the Grand River. But they did not own the land.   p. 7

Joseph Brant, the famous Mohawk Chief, was given a pension and land by the British near Burlington, where he built a log home. Joseph kept writing parts of the Bible in Mohawk before he died in 1807.   p. 8

Laura Ingersoll Secord
(1775 – 1868)

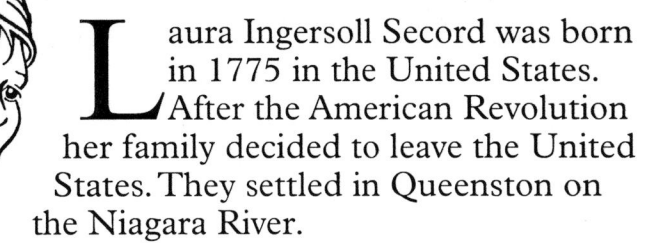

Laura Ingersoll Secord was born in 1775 in the United States. After the American Revolution her family decided to leave the United States. They settled in Queenston on the Niagara River.

In Queenston Laura met and married a young businessman named James Secord. Laura and James had five children and owned a successful store together.

The War of 1812 between Canada and the United States turned Laura's world upside down. On October 13, 1812, American soldiers rowed across the Niagara River and attacked the port of Queenston. Loud cannons woke Laura up. She quickly took her five children to a farmhouse. There they waited for news about James Secord who was fighting in the battle.

Soldiers passing by the house told Laura that James had been wounded. Laura ran to the battlefield and searched until she found him. He had been shot twice and could not walk. Suddenly three American soldiers appeared. They pushed Laura aside and started to beat James. Laura threw herself across James to protect him. An American officer who was standing nearby heard her screams and came to help. He ordered James to be carried home.

The Battle of Queenston was won by Canadian forces but the Secords were ruined. Their home and store had been robbed.

Queenston was invaded again the next May. This time the Americans won the battle. All of the Canadian men were marched away as prisoners. James Secord was allowed to stay because his war wounds prevented him from walking. The city was now controlled by American soldiers who needed places to live. Three American officers moved into the Secord house. Laura had to prepare meals every day for the officers.

Laura Ingersoll Secord

During one of these meals, Laura overheard the officers talking. They were planning a surprise attack. It was to take place the next night near a place called Beaver Dam. Laura decided to do her part for her adopted country. She would warn the Canadian army that the Americans were coming.

The next day at four in the morning, Laura began her dangerous 32-kilometre walk to Beaver Dam. She dressed in one of her good dresses and carried a basket with jam and bread. Laura told the American soldier gaurding her house she was going to visit her sick brother. The soldier let her pass.

Laura visited her sick brother and then continued on her way. Her 20-year-old niece, Elizabeth, joined her. The two women left the main road to avoid American soldiers. Laura and Elizabeth made their way through an area called the Black Swamp. The swamp was full of rattlesnakes, wolves, wildcats, and bears. The ground was soft and boggy. Often the women's feet sank into the bog and they had to pull themselves out using tree branches. Laura lost one of her shoes.

When they finally got out of the swamp, time was running out. They still had to climb the Niagara Escarpment. Known locally as the "Mountain", the escarpment was a long, high ridge of land. The slopes were steep and covered in forests.

Elizabeth Secord was too exhausted to go on so Laura continued alone. Twice she had to cross the winding and swollen Ten Mile Creek. During her first crossing she lost her other shoe. The rough ground cut her feet. She wrapped her bleeding feet with strips of cloth ripped from her petticoat.

Laura finally reached the top of the "Mountain". She stumbled out of the woods into a clearing. She found herself surrounded by Natives who were allies of the Canadian and British forces. Exhausted and terrified, she convinced them to take her to the commander.

Laura told the commander her story and he prepared for the Americans' surprise attack. The Canadians won a victorious battle.

After the battle, the commander was praised for his efforts but Laura Secord was forgotten. Fifty years later, she finally received recognition for her heroic walk. Her story was told in a newspaper article and Prince Edward in England sent Laura 100 pounds as a reward for her bravery.

Laura Ingersoll Secord died in 1868 at the age of 93. She is one of Canada's best known heroes.

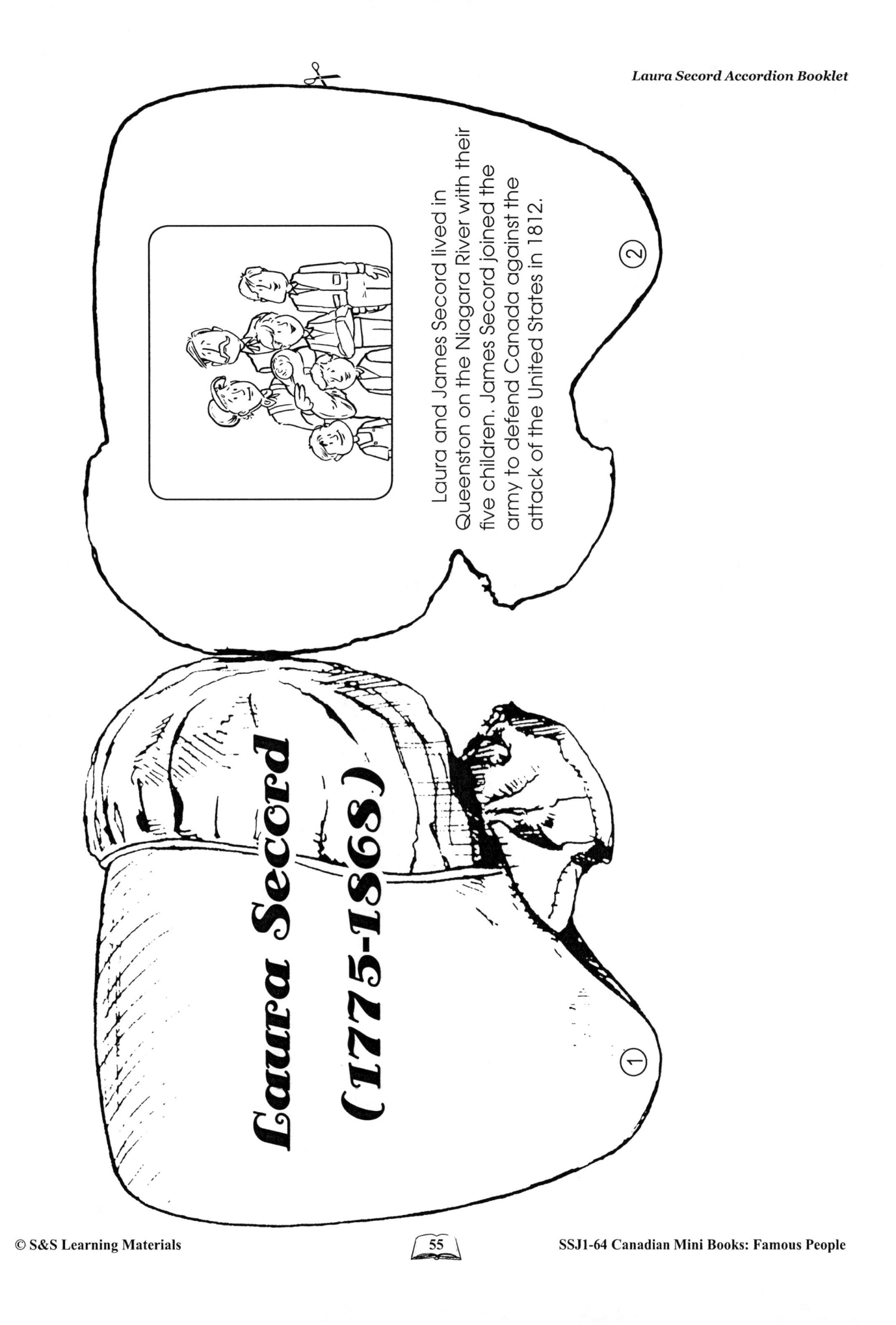

Laura and James Secord lived in Queenston on the Niagara River with their five children. James Secord joined the army to defend Canada against the attack of the United States in 1812.

②

Laura Secord (1775-1868)

①

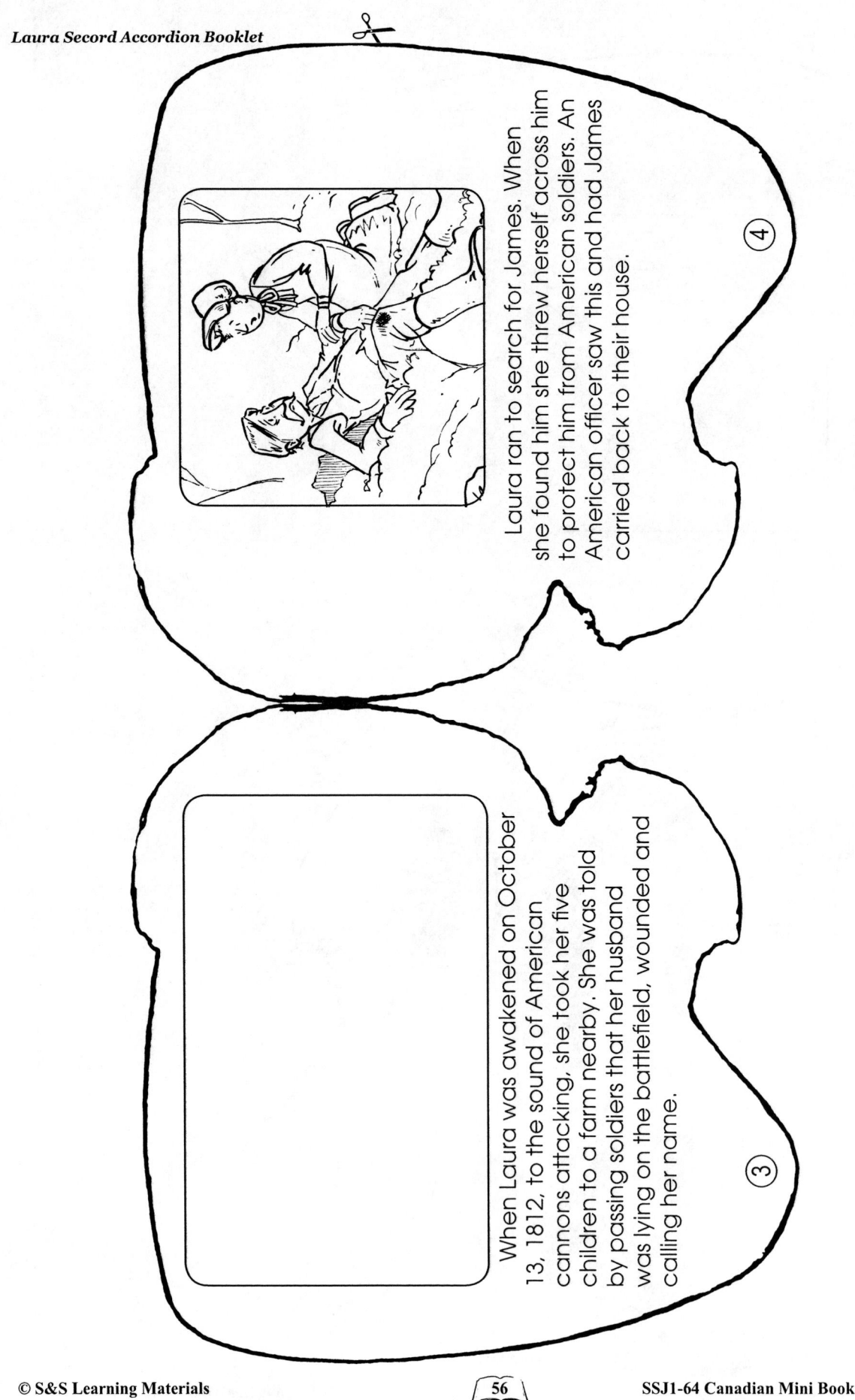

Laura ran to search for James. When she found him she threw herself across him to protect him from American soldiers. An American officer saw this and had James carried back to their house.

④

When Laura was awakened on October 13, 1812, to the sound of American cannons attacking, she took her five children to a farm nearby. She was told by passing soldiers that her husband was lying on the battlefield, wounded and calling her name.

③

Dressed in good shoes, a cloak, and a bonnet, and carrying a basket of food, Laura told the guard that she was going to visit her sick brother.

⑥

Three American officers moved into the Secords' house while planning more battles. Laura overheard them talking. They were planning a surprise attack on the British at a place called Beaver Dam. She decided she had to warn the British.

⑦

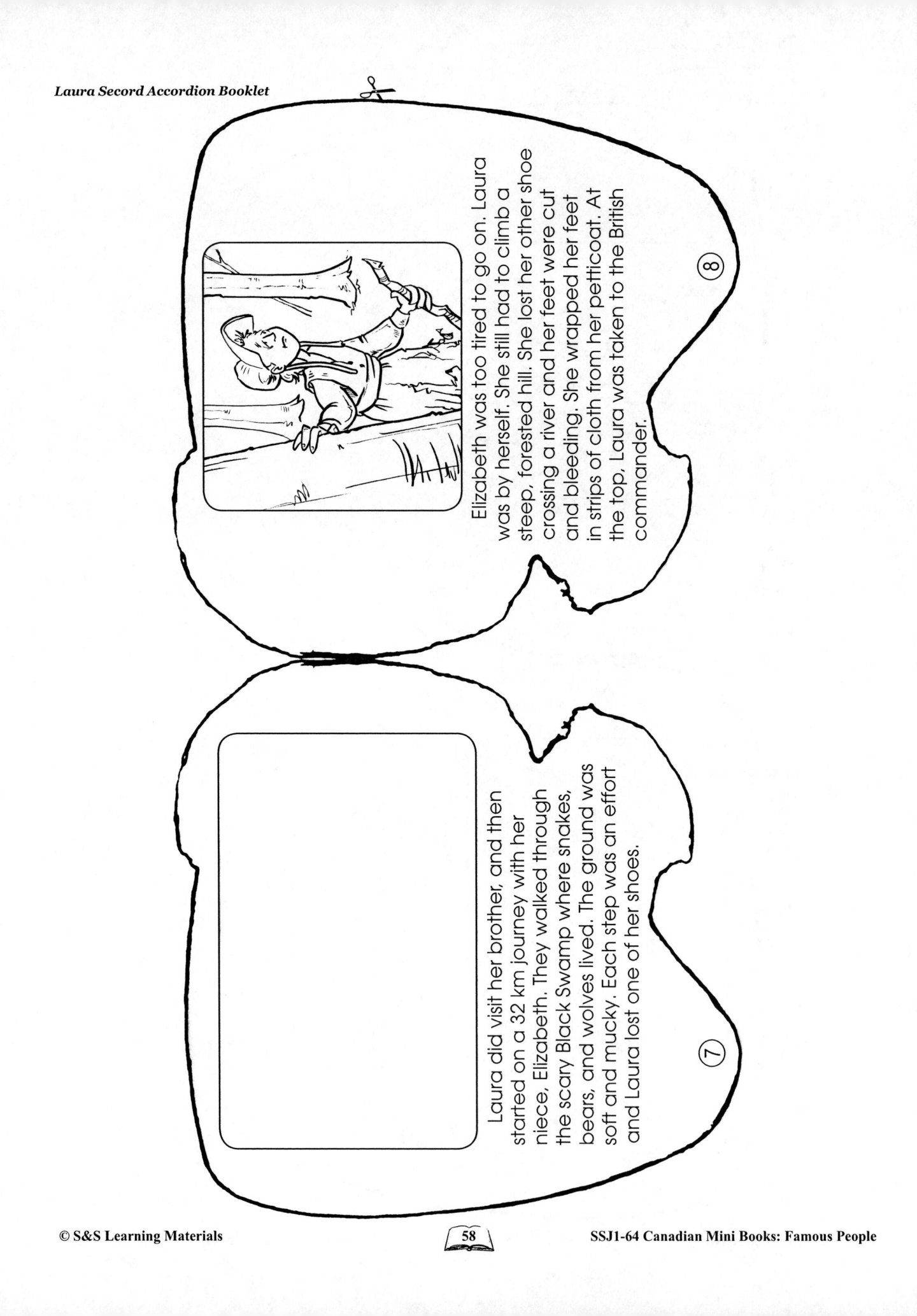

Elizabeth was too tired to go on. Laura was by herself. She still had to climb a steep, forested hill. She lost her other shoe crossing a river and her feet were cut and bleeding. She wrapped her feet in strips of cloth from her petticoat. At the top, Laura was taken to the British commander.

⑧

Laura did visit her brother, and then started on a 32 km journey with her niece, Elizabeth. They walked through the scary Black Swamp where snakes, bears, and wolves lived. The ground was soft and mucky. Each step was an effort and Laura lost one of her shoes.

⑦

After the battle, Laura returned to Queenston where people kept quiet about her bravery so that the Americans wouldn't return to kill them. The Secords were now very poor, as James was so wounded from the war that he couldn't do a lot of work.

⑩

When Laura told the shocked commander about the surprise attack, he prepared to surprise the Americans instead. Two days later, the Americans lost the battle at Beaver Dam.

⑨

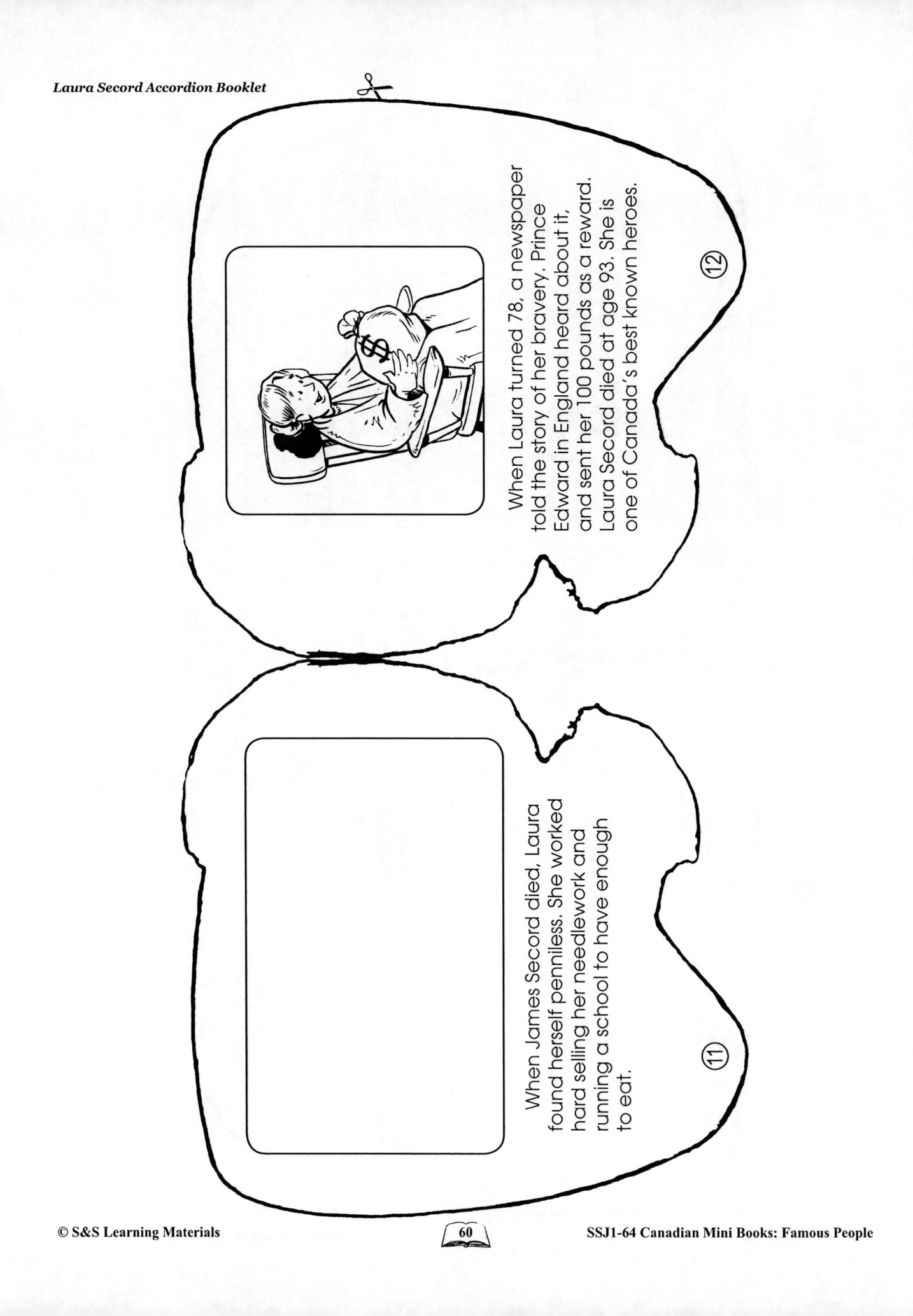

When Laura turned 78, a newspaper told the story of her bravery. Prince Edward in England heard about it, and sent her 100 pounds as a reward. Laura Secord died at age 93. She is one of Canada's best known heroes.

⑫

When James Secord died, Laura found herself penniless. She worked hard selling her needlework and running a school to have enough to eat.

⑪

Sir John A. Macdonald
(1815 – 1891)

John Alexander Macdonald was born in Scotland in 1815. When he was five years old, John and his family moved to Canada. They were hoping to find a better life in the New World. They settled near Kingston in Upper Canada (now Ontario).

John's mother wanted her son to receive a good education. The family was poor but they scraped together enough money to send John to boarding school. He developed a love for reading and became well informed on many topics. After school John worked as a lawyer. He was admired for his knowledge, his friendly manner, and his sense of humour.

In 1844 John was elected to the government of Upper Canada. He worked very hard to get the British colonies to join together and form a confederation. Canada finally became a country in 1867. Macdonald was appointed the first Prime Minister. Queen Victoria rewarded him with a knighthood and he became Sir John A. MacDonald.

Macdonald fell from power in 1873 but was re-elected a few years later. He remained Prime Minister for three more terms. Macdonald continued to build the new nation of Canada. He brought Manitoba, the Northwest Territories, British Columbia, and Prince Edward Island into the Confederation. He also created an economic program called the National Policy and oversaw completion of the Canadian Pacific Railway. The railway was an important link between Canadians living across huge distances.

Sir John A. Macdonald died of a stroke on June 6, 1891, when he was still Prime Minister. He is remembered as the "Father of Confederation".

④ Growing up

Even though John's family was poor, they felt that learning was important. They saved money and sent John to school in Kingston. He studied many things like math, history, Latin, and French.

Working as a Lawyer ⑤

At age 15, John went to work in a law office. At night he studied so he could open his own law office. Because he was fair, smart, and friendly, the people of Kingston elected him leader of Canada West.

③ Home Sweet Home!

The Macdonald family settled in a small community near Kingston in Upper Canada. Here, John's father ran a mill and built their home.

Arriving in Canada ②

When the ship landed in Quebec City, John was so excited he was the first one off the ship. This young boy would eventually change Canada for all time...

 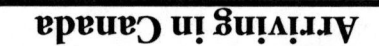

⑥ **One Big Country?**

First Prime Minister of Canada ⑦

In 1864, John A. Macdonald told all the leaders at a big meeting in Charlottetown that the colonies should work as one: his idea for joining together was called Confederation.

John A. Macdonald was chosen as Canada's first Prime Minister in 1867 because he had worked very hard to bring about Confederation. Queen Victoria made him a knight, and changed his name to Sir John A. Macdonald.

---

① Sir John A. Macdonald 1815-1891

John Alexander Macdonald was born near Glasgow, Scotland on January 10, 1815. In 1820, his poor family left with other immigrants to travel by ship to a new land.

Father of Confederation ⑧

Sir John A. Macdonald is remembered as the founder of Canada. He also joined the country from coast to coast with the Canadian railway. He died while still Prime Minister in 1891.

Harriet Tubman Davis
(1820 – 1913)

Harriet Tubman Davis was born a slave in the United States in 1820. She grew up hating slavery and fought against it her entire life. At the age of 15, Harriet refused to help tie up a slave who had tried to escape. An angry overseer hit her on the head with an iron weight. It knocked her unconscious for many days. For the rest of her life Harriet suffered from blinding headaches and frequently fell asleep at any time for no reason.

When Harriet was 30 years old, she learned that her family was being sold to a plantation further south where slaves were treated even worse. She decided to escape and headed north by the Underground Railroad.

The Underground Railroad had very little to do with trains. It was made up of brave people who secretly helped escaped slaves. These people were called "conductors". They housed and fed the runaways and guided them to the next conductor. Churches, houses, and barns were used as secret "railway stations" or places to hide slaves.

Harriet decided to become a conductor so she could go back south and rescue her family. Members of the Underground Railroad didn't think women could be conductors but Harriet knew they were wrong. She bought herself a gun and became the most successful conductor of them all. Harriet rescued her parents and four of her brothers as well as 300 other slaves.

In 1850, the United States passed a new law. It said that runaway slaves in free states could be hunted down and returned to their owners. Canada was now the only place where slaves could live in freedom. Harriet moved to St. Catherine's in Canada West (Ontario) and all routes of the Underground Railway were directed into Canada.

Harriet Tubman Davis never lost a passenger nor was she ever captured. She was a dedicated woman who fought very hard for the freedom of her people.

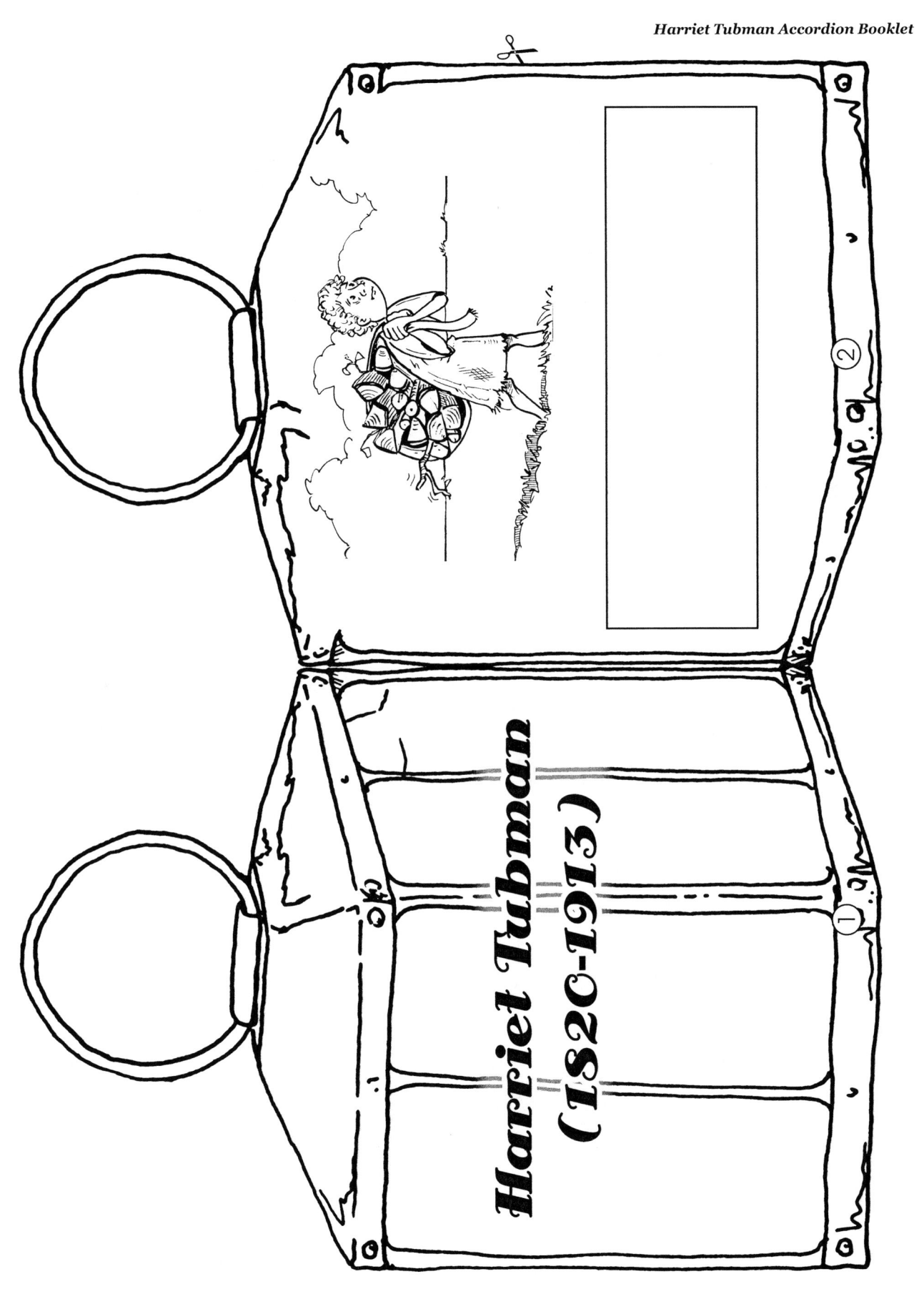

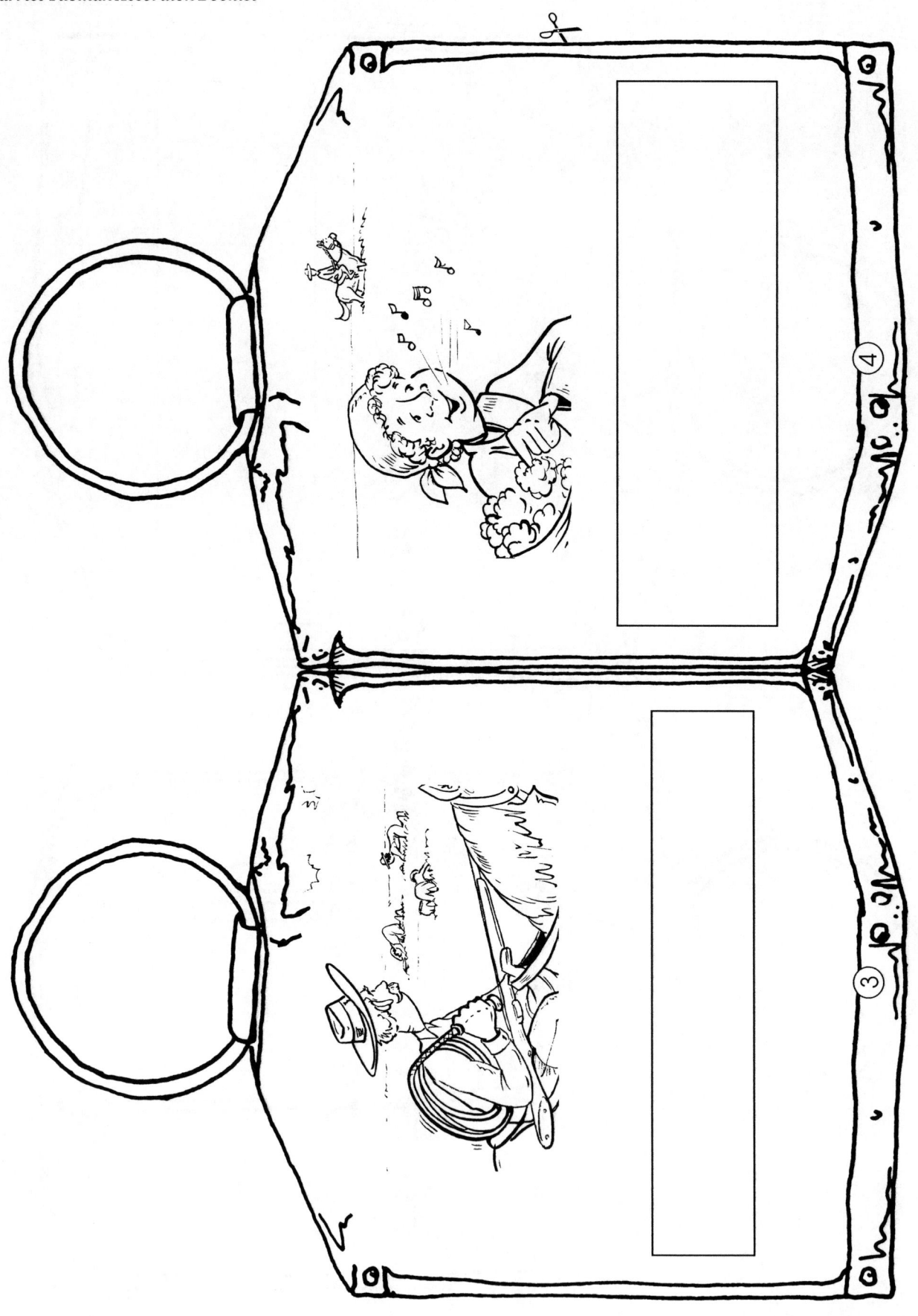

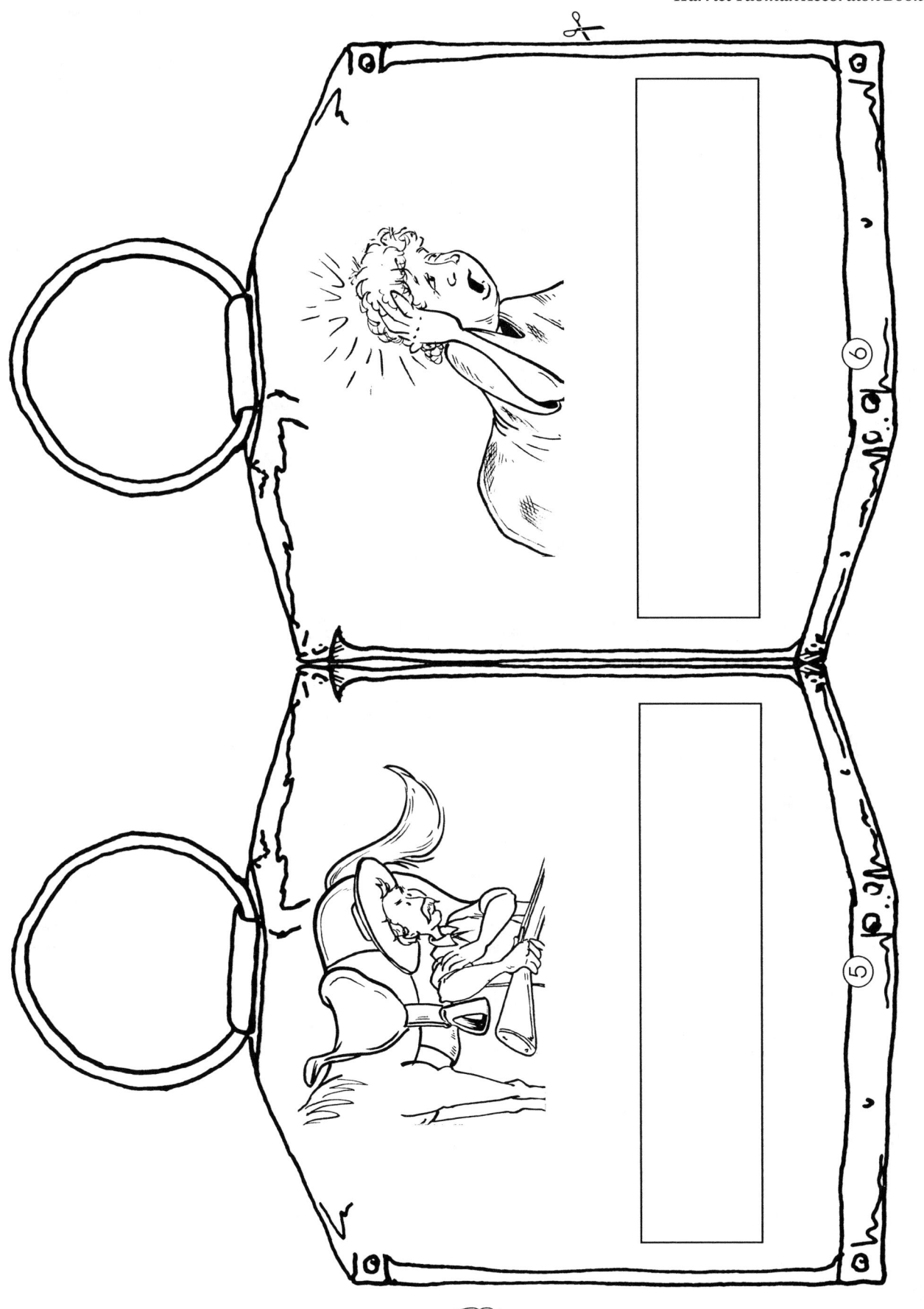

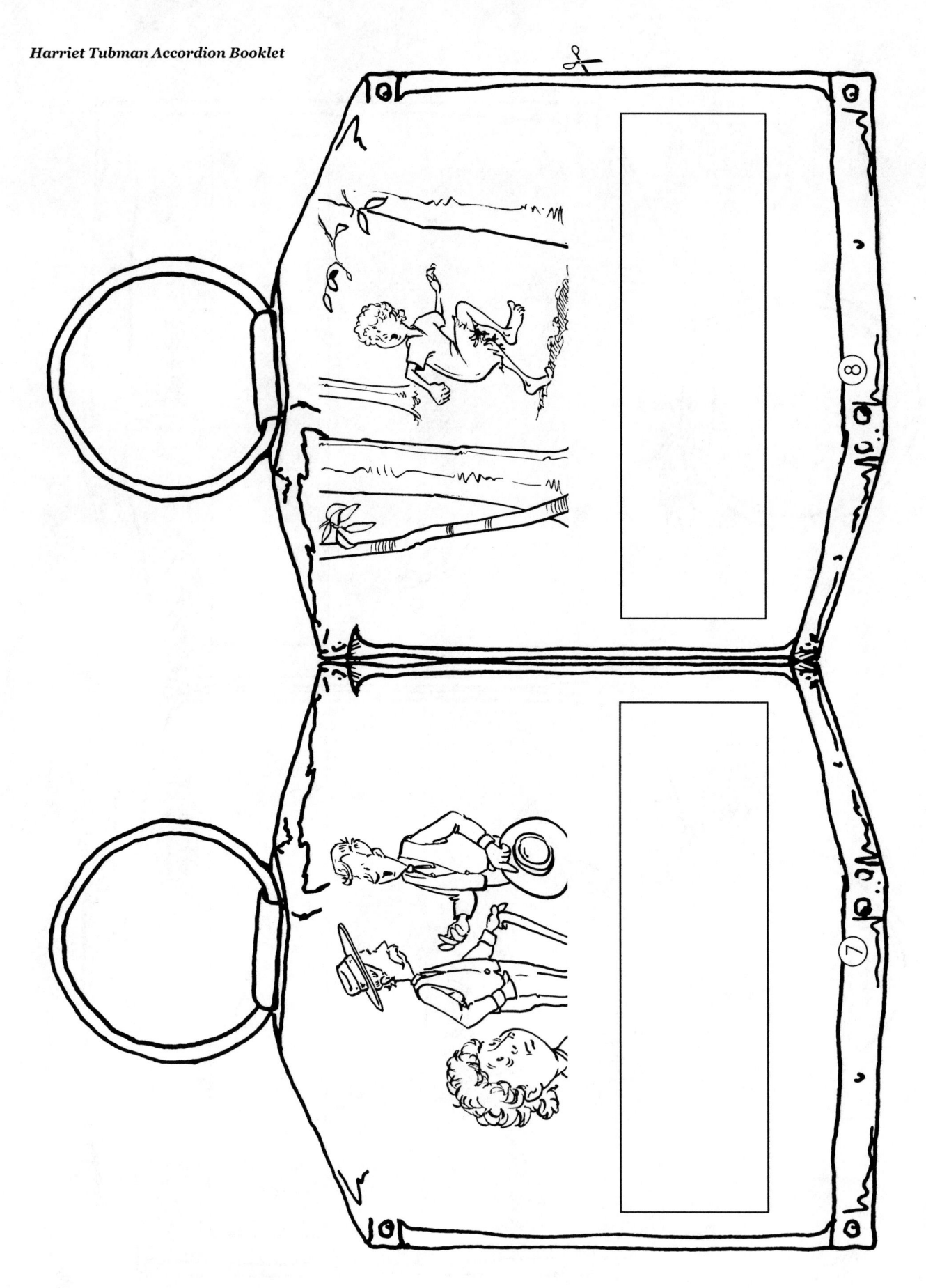

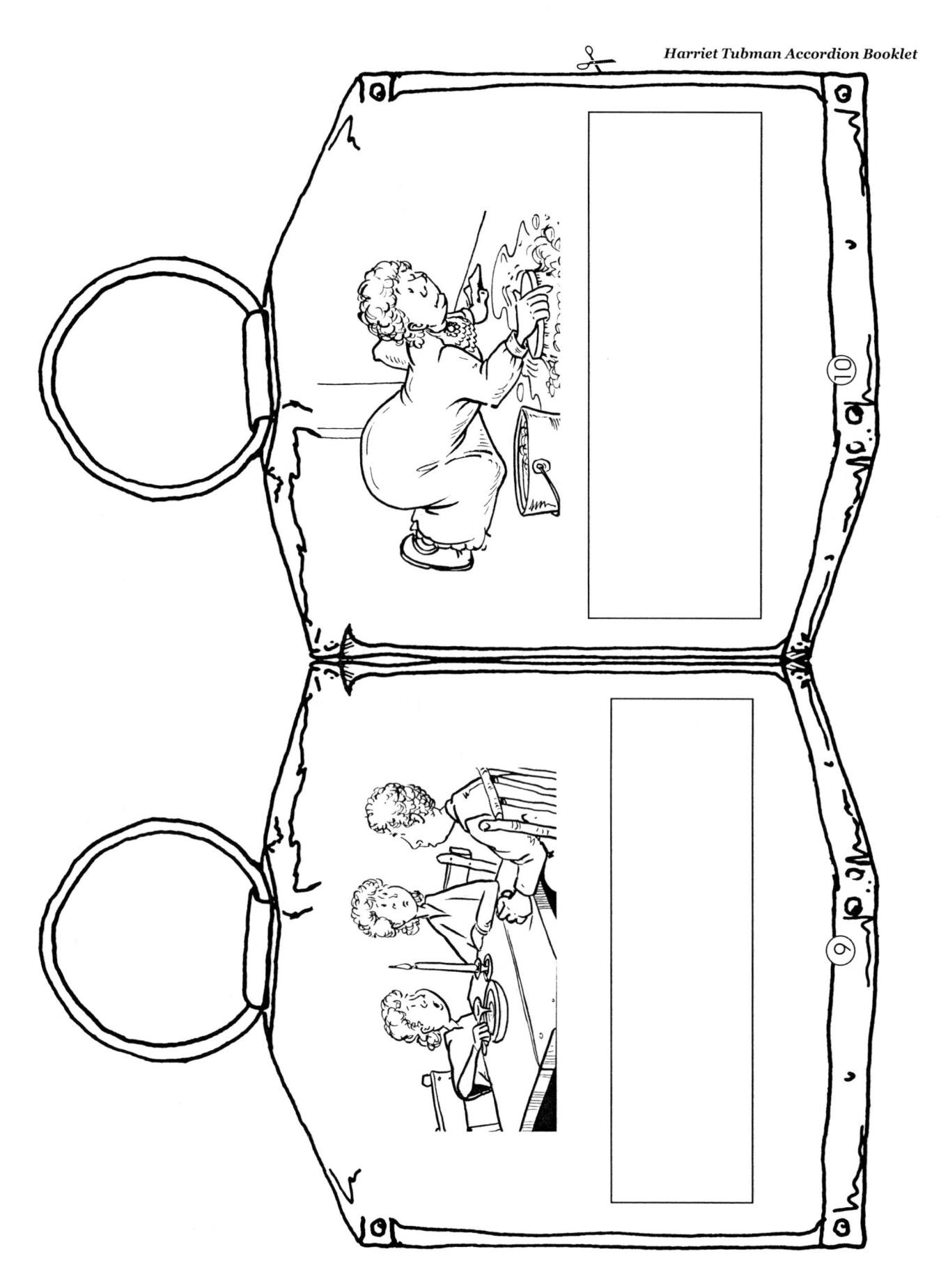

Harriet Tubman Accordion Booklet

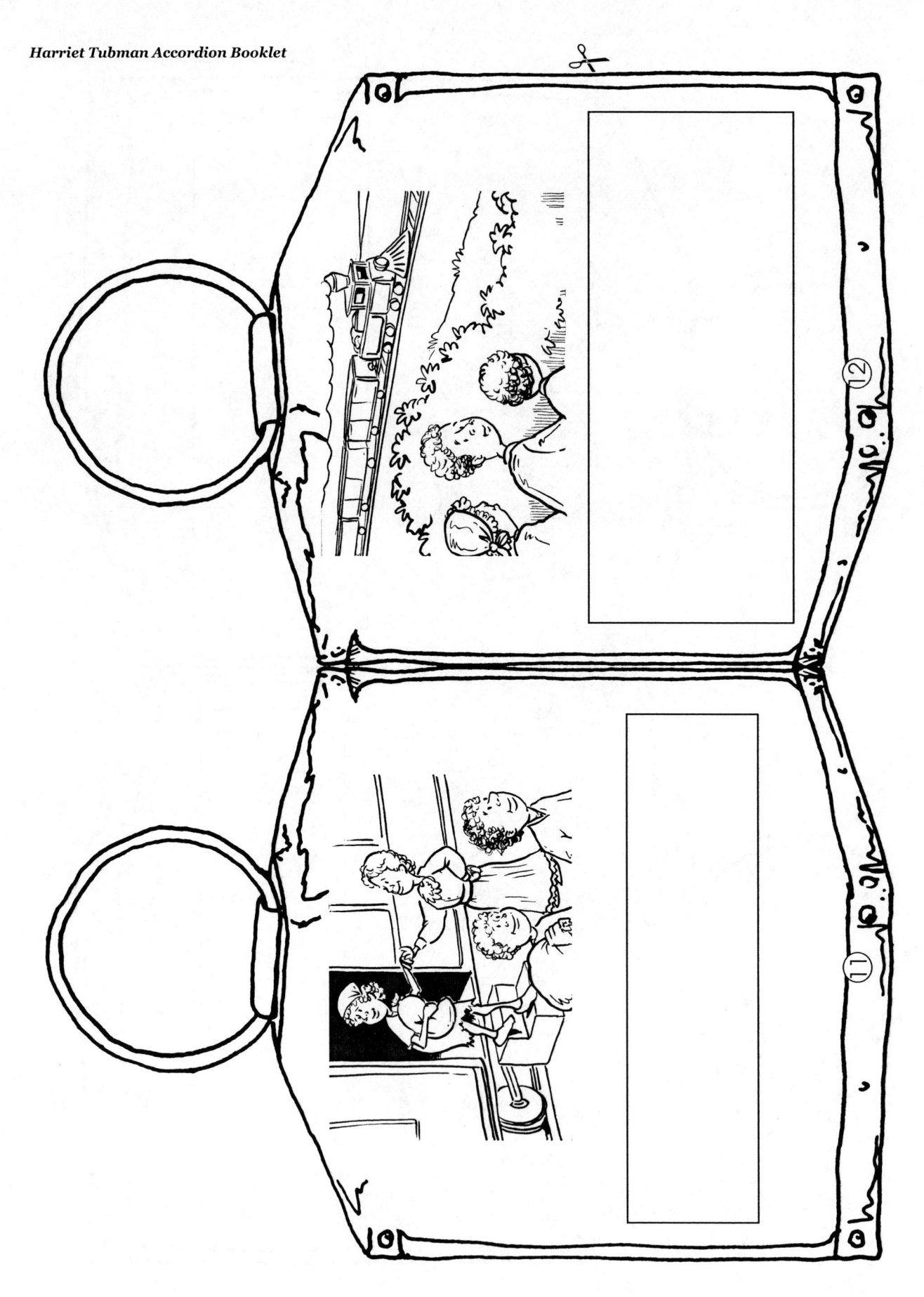

Harriet Tubman Davis was born a slave on a plantation in the United States. At age seven she was made to work as a field hand. From sunup to sundown she hoed the ground, split firewood, and cut hay. (2)

As the slaves worked, an overseer or boss watched them carefully to make sure that no one tried to escape. (3)

Often the overseer made the slaves sing. He felt that quiet slaves were thinking about how to run away. No one knew that in their songs, the slaves were singing hidden messages. (4)

When Harriet was 15 years old she helped another slave escape from the plantation. The overseer was very angry and hit Harriet on her head very hard. (5)

For the rest of her life, Harriet had a dent in her head and had painful headaches. She would also fall asleep for no reason while she was working or talking. (6)

One day Harriet overheard the overseer talking to the plantation owner about selling Harriet's family to a plantation in the south. She knew that slaves were treated even worse there. (7)

Harriet had heard that slaves were free in the north and in Canada. One night she escaped from the plantation with the help of a group of people called the Underground Railway. (8)

Harriet enjoyed her freedom but missed her family. She learned more about the Underground Railway and how "conductors" often went back to get their families. (9)

The people of the Underground Railway told Harriet that women could not be conductors but Harriet knew better. She worked hard at many jobs to make enough money to buy a gun. Harriet soon became the best conductor of all. (10)

Harriet rescued her parents and four brothers as well as 300 other slaves without harm coming to anyone. Harriet was very dedicated to the fight for freedom. (11)

In 1850, an American law said that runaway slaves living in the free states would be hunted down and returned to their owners. Harriet Tubman moved to St. Catherines, Ontario. All the routes of the Underground Railway were changed to lead to Canada where slaves could live in freedom. (12)

Nellie Mooney McClung
(1873-1951)

Nellie Mooney McClung was born in 1873 in Chatsworth, Ontario. When Nellie was seven her family moved to the Souris Valley in Manitoba. At the age of 16 Nelly became a teacher. When Nellie got off the train she was told that hail had flattened the crops. There would be no money for her salary. A local family gave Nellie room and board while she taught.

At 23 Nellie married a man named Wesley McClung. They had five children together. It was Nellie's mother-in-law who encouraged her to begin writing. Nelly's first novel was called *Sowing Seeds in Danny*. It became a national bestseller.

Nellie was happy with her life but she was disturbed by the hardship she saw in other women's lives. In the 1800s, a woman was not a person in the eyes of the law. Everything a woman owned, even her clothes, belonged by law to her husband. Any money she earned or inherited was her husband's. A woman's husband even owned their children. He made all the decisions about their upbringing. He could even leave them to someone else in his will when their mother was still alive to look after them. There were no laws to stop a husband from treating his family badly.

Alcohol made life even more difficult for many women in the 1800s. Women were discouraged from drinking but men drank heavily and often went home drunk. They were free to spend all their wages in local taverns and then hurt their wives and children in drunken anger. Women and children living with such men had no laws to protect them. They had no one to turn to for help. Without the right to vote, they could not pressure the government to create new laws.

Women began to fight against the hardship caused by drinking. A group of women organized The Women's Christian Temperance Union. The Union wanted all alcohol banned. Nellie McClung spoke at her first Temperance meeting when she read aloud from her novel, *Sowing Seeds in Danny*. It was clear right away she was a powerful public speaker.

Nellie Mooney McClung

Politics were often discussed at the Temperance meetings. Nellie and others felt that women needed the right to vote so they could push for laws to make Canada a better place to live. The women who fought for the right to vote were called suffragists or suffragettes.

Nellie wrote and spoke in favour of women's right to vote. She spoke at over 400 public meetings. Sometimes she spoke three times a day. Her speaking tours took her across Canada, the United States, and England. Nellie became famous but her audiences were not always friendly. Some people criticized her and called her names.

Gradually more people became convinced that women should have the right to vote. When T.C. Norris was elected as the new Premier of Manitoba, the suffragists rejoiced. Norris had promised to support voting rights for women.

Unfortunately Norris did not keep his word. He said he would not introduce a suffrage bill into Parliament unless they could show there was popular support for it. The suffragists accepted the challenge. They collected over 40,000 signatures on a petition. In 1916 women in Manitoba finally won the right to vote. They could also run for political office.

Nellie McClung was not in Manitoba for the celebration. She and her family had moved to Edmonton, Alberta. In Alberta she campaigned for old age pensions, better working conditions in factories, minimum wage, easier divorces, and a ban of alcohol. She was elected as a Liberal member of the Alberta government in 1921. Nellie lost her second election in 1926 by 60 votes because she supported the alcohol ban.

Nellie did not let the defeat bother her. She became involved with the "Persons Case". This was a protest against the wording of the British North American Act of 1867. Under the Act, the word "persons" referred only to men. This meant that women were not "persons" under the law. Along with four other prominent Canadian women, Nellie helped get the interpretation of the Act changed. Women finally became "persons" in the eyes of the law. They could now become Senators and hold other important positions.

Nellie Mooney McClung continued her writing career after she left politics. She wrote 16 books in all. In 1951, Nellie McClung died at the age of 78. She will be forever remembered for making Canada a better place to live for women and all Canadians.

④ **Nellie, the Public Speaker**

⑤ **Nellie, the Law Changer**

③ **Nellie, the Writer**

② **Nellie, the School Teacher**

⑥ **Nellie, the Politician**

⑦ **Nellie, the "Person"**

① **Nellie McClung 1873-1951**

⑧ **Nellie, a Canadian Hero**

p.1
Nellie McClung was born in Ontario in 1873. When she was seven, she moved by ship, train, and ox-cart with her family to Manitoba. There she grew up on her family's farm and went to school.

p.2
When Nellie was 16 years old she became a teacher. The people could not pay her but she was able to live with a family in the community.

p.3
Nellie worried about the way women and children were treated. She wrote her thoughts and feelings every day in her diary. This led to her first book called "Sewing Seeds for Danny".

p.4
Nellie began speaking at meetings. She was very popular. Sometimes people were rude and made fun of her dreams to have new laws to protect women and children.

p.5
Nellie knew that in order to have new laws passed, women needed to be able to vote. In 1916, the Manitoba government gave women the right to vote. Canada gave women the right to vote a few years later.

p.6
Nellie McClung, at age 48, was elected as a member of the provincial government in Alberta. She wanted to get laws passed to help people. She worked for money to help the elderly, for better places for people to work, for higher wages, and many other things.

p.7
Nellie and a group of women had the law changed that said that women were not "persons". At that time women could not hold important jobs in the government. Today many women hold important jobs in government.

p.8
Nellie Mooney McClung will be remembered for her 16 books and her interest in people and for making Canada a better place to live, especially for women and children.

FAMOUS CANADIANS IN HISTORY

Leif Eriksson

1. From where did Leif Eriksson come?

   _____

2. Where did he explore?

   _____

3. What was Leif's major contribution to Canada?

   _____

   _____

4. Was the Viking colony worth the effort? Explain why or why not.

   _____

   _____

   _____

Jacques Cartier

1. From where did Jacques Cartier come?

   _____

2. Where did he explore?

   _____

3. When was he in Canada exploring?

   _____

4. What could Cartier have done differently to have a better

   relationship with the Natives?_____

   _____

   _____

FAMOUS CANADIANS IN HISTORY

Samuel de Champlain

1. From where did Samuel de Champlain come?

   _____

2. Where did he explore?

   _____

3. When was he exploring?

   _____

4. Do you think Champlain's nickname of "Father of New France" was appropriate?_____

   _____

   _____

James Wolfe

1. What was James Wolfe's job?

   _____

2. Why did he become famous?_____

   _____

3. When was his most famous battle?

   _____

4. What was his major contribution to Canada?_____

   _____

   _____

   _____

FAMOUS CANADIANS IN HISTORY

Louis-Joseph de Montcalm

1. From where did Montcalm come?

    _____

2. Where did Montcalm die?

    _____

3. What did he do to become well-known?

    _____

    _____

4. What could Montcalm have changed to win the war with Wolfe
    and the British?_____

    _____

Joseph Brant

1. Who was Joseph Brant?

    _____

2. Where did he go to school?

    _____

3. Describe a connection you have to Joseph Brant.

    _____

    _____

4. How do you feel about the British breaking their promise to
    Brant and giving the Iroquois land to the United States?

    _____

    _____

FAMOUS CANADIANS IN HISTORY

Laura Second

1. Who was Laura Secord?

   _____

2. What did she do to become famous?

   _____

3. Describe a connection you have to Laura Secord.

   _____

   _____

4. Was Laura Secord a real Canadian heroine? Tell why.

   _____

   _____

Harriet Tubman

1. Where was Harriet Tubman born?

   _____

2. Was Harriet brave? Tell how you know.

   _____

   _____

3. Describe a connection you have to Harriet Tubman.

   _____

4. Judge whether Harriet was right to help slaves escape when it meant going against the laws of her country. _____

   _____

FAMOUS CANADIANS IN HISTORY

Sir John A. Macdonald

1. Where did Sir John A. Macdonald live?

   _____

2. What was his job?

   _____

3. What did he do to become well-known?

   _____

   _____

4. Prove that Sir John A. Macdonald was a great Prime Minister
   of Canada. _____

   _____

   _____

Nellie McClung

1. Where did Nellie McClung grow up?

   _____

2. When did the Manitoba government give women the right to vote?

   _____

3. What was Nellie's major contribution to Canada?

   _____

   _____

4. Was McClung's decision to fight to change the laws so women
   were "people" a good idea? Tell why. _____

   _____

   _____

Who Is It?

In the envelope are some pictures and name cards of famous people.

Match the name card with the picture card of each famous person.

Example:

Laura Secord

Why Am I Famous?

In the envelope are some name cards and sentence cards about famous people.

Read the sentence card carefully.

Match the name of the person to each sentence.

Example:

His people were the first Europeans to find North America.

Leif Eriksson

Recognizing historical people: Cut out the pictures and name cards. Mount them on a sturdy backing and laminate. Store the name and picture cards in an envelope. Attach the instruction card to the envelope.

		Sir John A. Macdonald
		Joseph Brant
		Laura Secord
		Jacques Cartier
		Samuel de Champlain
		Nellie McClung

Recognizing historical people: Cut out the pictures and name cards. Mount them on a sturdy backing and laminate. Store the name and picture cards in an envelope. Attach the instruction card to the envelope.

Why am I Famous? Matching historical figures to his/her importance: Cut out the name cards and sentence cards. Mount them on sturdy backing and laminate. Store the cards in an envelope. Attach the instruction card.

She worked on the Underground Railway and led many slaves to Canada.	Harriet Tubman
She worked hard to get women the right to vote.	Nellie McClung
His people were the first Europeans to find North America.	Leif Eriksson
He led his troops up a rocky cliff to defeat the French on the Plains of Abraham.	James Wolfe
He was a French leader who was defeated by James Wolfe and his army.	Louis-Joseph de Montcalm

Why am I Famous? Matching historical figures to his/her importance: Cut out the name cards and sentence cards. Mount them on sturdy backing and laminate. Store the cards in an envelope. Attach the instruction card.

He was the first Prime Minister of Canada.	Sir John A. Macdonald
She warned a British officer that the Americans were planning a surprise attack.	Laura Secord
He was a famous Mohawk Chief who helped the British.	Joseph Brant
He built a fort called the Habitation at Quebec.	Samuel de Champlain
He explored the St. Lawrence River and put a cross on the Gaspé Peninsula.	Jacques Cartier

Attach the instruction cards to envelopes.

Famous People Riddles

In the envelope are some riddle cards and name cards.

Read each riddle carefully.

Match the name cards to the riddle cards.

Example:

> I am a brave woman.
> I walked through a swamp.
> I climbed a rocky cliff.
>
> Who am I?

Laura Secord

Make History Sentences

In the envelope are some cards with sentence parts.

Use the cards to make good history sentences.

Example:

> Jacques Cartier sailed up

> the St. Lawrence River with his men.

Famous People Riddles-Recognizing historical people: Cut out the riddle cards and name cards. Mount them on a sturdy backing and laminate. Store the cards in an envelope. Attach the instruction card to the envelope.

I am a well-known woman. I rescued my husband from a battlefield. I walked far to warn of an American attack. Who am I?	**Laura Secord**
I am a British officer. I came to Canada to fight the French. I led my men up a steep cliff to capture Quebec. Who am I?	**James Wolfe**
I grew up near Kingston. I wanted the colonies to become one country. I was Canada's first Prime Minister. Who am I?	**Sir John A. Macdonald**
I am a famous French explorer. On the Gaspé Peninsula I put up a cross. I visited Native villages on my trips. Who am I?	**Jacques Cartier**
My people were the first Europeans to find North America. We built a village in Newfoundland. We made houses out of stone and earth. Who am I?	**Leif Eriksson**

Famous People Riddles-Recognizing historical people: Cut out the riddle cards and name cards. Mount them on a sturdy backing and laminate. Store the cards in an envelope. Attach the instruction card to the envelope.

I was a famous Mohawk Chief. I led the Six Nations to help the British fight the Americans. Who am I?	**Joseph Brant**
I grew up in Manitoba. I was a teacher. I believed women should be able to vote. Who am I?	**Nellie McClung**
When I was young I was a slave. I escaped. I worked on the Underground Railway helping other slaves escape, too. Who am I?	**Harriet Tubman**
I was a French explorer. I built a fort at Quebec called the Habitation. I lived with the Hurons for a winter. Who am I?	**Samuel de Champlain**
I was the French commander of Quebec. I led my men into battle with the British. We lost the battle. Who am I?	**Louis-Joseph de Montcalm**

Making History Sentences: Cut out the sentence cards. Mount the cards on a sturdy backing and laminate. Store the sentence cards in an envelope. Attach the instruction card.

For three months James Wolfe	attacked Quebec with his cannons.
Samuel de Champlain started the	"Order of Good Cheer" at Port Royal.
Harriet Tubman was a conductor	on the Underground Railway.
Nellie McClung did not like how	women and children were treated.
Joseph Brant was an officer	in the British Army.
Leif Eriksson was a Viking	explorer who visited Canada.
Jacques Cartier took Donnacona's	sons to France.
Sir John A. Macdonald is often	called the "Father of Confederation".
Laura Secord walked 32	kilometres to warn the British that the Americans were coming
Montcalm rode a black horse	when he led his men into battle.

Name that Famous Person

Name:_____

Print the correct name of each famous person on the
line provided in the sentences below.

Laura Secord	Harriet Tubman	Louis-Joseph de Montcalm
Nellie McClung	Leif Eriksson	Sir John A. Macdonald
James Wolfe	Jacques Cartier	Samuel de Champlain
	Joseph Brant	

1. _____walked through a swamp and climbed a steep cliff to reach the British.

2. _____explored the St. Lawrence River and visited two Native villages.

3. John A. Macdonald was given a knighthood by Queen Victoria and was then called_____.

4. _____translated parts of the Bible into Mohawk.

5. _____built the first European settlement in Newfoundland.

6. _____was a pale, sickly boy who became a famous British commander.

7. _____did not want to become a soldier but joined the army because his family expected him to.

8. _____dressed like a man and carried a gun while she rescued slaves from plantations.

9. _____learned many new things while he lived with the Hurons one winter.

10. _____worked very hard to get a law passed that gave women the right to vote.

Search for the Famous Person

Name:_____

Samuel de Champlain

Louis-Joseph de Montcalm

Laura Secord

Harriet Tubman

Jacques Cartier

Nellie McClung

The Vikings

James Wolfe

Joseph Brant

Sir John A. Macdonald

L	C	A	S	A	O	B	M	E	A	A	M	C	S	A	M	E	S	E	R
O	A	E	E	U	U	J	O	S	E	P	H	B	R	A	N	T	A	I	L
U	A	R	N	L	I	L	O	S	T	E	A	K	U	L	E	A	E	L	A
I	H	H	S	I	N	I	H	A	S	A	O	I	I	A	L	I	E	A	L
S	I	R	J	O	H	N	A	M	A	C	D	O	N	A	L	D	B	M	N
J	H	J	S	J	A	C	Q	U	E	S	C	A	R	T	I	E	R	H	E
O	L	L	A	U	R	A	S	E	C	O	R	D	M	S	E	U	L	R	E
S	E	J	L	A	R	Q	R	L	I	P	A	N	P	M	M	A	H	O	L
E	E	O	O	G	I	D	R	D	E	A	M	N	C	P	C	L	N	U	A
P	T	O	U	E	E	A	R	E	E	Q	U	M	A	M	C	P	D	S	M
H	A	E	P	T	T	E	E	C	A	U	R	L	E	R	L	E	B	H	M
D	E	R	I	O	T	L	G	H	A	O	C	C	S	C	U	H	T	G	T
E	U	O	S	E	U	H	A	A	M	D	N	L	U	U	N	G	L	S	R
M	W	O	N	Q	B	P	C	M	H	E	H	G	I	J	G	G	J	O	L
O	N	I	A	I	M	A	T	P	U	S	I	I	H	O	C	D	S	O	W
N	E	D	I	E	A	L	J	L	O	A	E	D	S	F	U	W	A	E	M
T	N	P	E	J	N	A	J	A	M	E	S	W	O	L	F	E	A	L	E
C	J	H	D	A	B	F	A	I	G	S	I	H	E	I	E	T	T	P	U
A	T	H	E	V	I	K	I	N	G	S	A	D	P	G	C	C	M	P	A
L	H	C	F	C	A	H	H	A	N	M	E	E	H	R	C	N	L	R	I
M	T	J	D	O	S	P	M	Y	E	H	A	O	T	W	E	B	M	U	D

Famous Person Crossword Puzzle

Famous Person Crossword Puzzle Clues

Read the Crossword Puzzle clues carefully.

Across

1. Louis-Joseph de Montcalm was the commander of this town.
2. Samuel de Champlain and Jacques Cartier were famous French_____.
3. These brave men and women sailed across the Atlantic Ocean and discovered North America.
4. Nellie McClung wanted all women in Canada to be able to _____during elections.
5. Jacques Cartier named this town.
6. Laura Secord overheard American soldiers planning a surprise _____.
7. James Wolfe and Louis-Joseph de Montcalm were brave _____.

Down

1. Sir John A. Macdonald was knighted by this royal lady.
2. Joseph Brant was a famous Chief of this tribe.
3. Harriet Tubman fought against_____ her whole life.
4. This woman received a gift from Prince Edward because of her bravery.

Answer Key

Famous Canadians in History *(page 77)*

Leif Eriksson
1. Greenland   2. Newfoundland (Baffin Island too)
3. He was the first European to discover Canada.
4. Answers will vary (e.g., the colony was worth the effort because they found new land).

Jacques Cartier
1. France
2. Newfoundland, Labrador, and the St. Lawrence River (Gaspé Peninsula too)
3. 1534-1539 (1500s)
4. Answers will vary (e.g., the kidnapped the Native Chiefs and their sons; this was not a nice thing to do).

Samuel de Champlain
1. France   2. Quebec, Ontario (Lake Huron, Lake Champlain)
3. 1604-1616 (1600s)
4. Answers will vary (e.g., yes, this is a good nickname because he made the first French settlement, and he looked after the people too).

James Wolfe
1. soldier (General also acceptable)
2. He won a battle against the French at Quebec City.
3. 1759
4. Answers will vary (e.g., the helped make Canada English, not just French).

Louis-Joseph de Montcalm
1. France
2. Canada (Quebec City)
3. Answers will vary (e.g., he was the leader of the French in the battle against the British, he lost).
4. Answers will vary (e.g., he could have stayed inside the walls of Quebec City).

Joseph Brant
1. a Mohawk Chief   2. a British school
3. Answers will vary (e.g., I like to read).   4. Answers will vary (e.g., angry and sad).

Laura Secord
1. wife of a soldier who lived in Ontario
2. She walked 32 kilometres to warn the British of an American attack.
3. Answers will vary (e.g., I have walked in a swamp and lost my shoe, too).
4. Answers will vary (e.g., yes she is because she was very brave and she helped stop Canada from becoming part of America).

Harriet Tubman
1. on a plantation in the United States
2. Answers will vary (e.g., Harriet was brave because she escaped and she risked her life to help people).
3. Answers will vary (e.g., I know what it is like to be scared too).
4. Answers will vary (e.g., yes it was right because slavery is very wrong even if the law says it is not).

Sir John A. Macdonald
1. near Kingston   2. lawyer
3. Answers will vary (e.g., he pulled all of the provinces and territories together to form a country; he also formed a new railroad that went from coast to coast).
4. Answers will vary (e.g., he kept all the different people in Canada's provinces together).

Nellie Mcclung
1. Manitoba   2. 1916
3. Answers will vary (e.g., she helped to make Canada a better place to live, especially for women and children).
4. Answers will vary (e.g., women are people just like men are; they are a little different, but just as smart and just as good).

Name that Famous Person *(page 91)*

1. Laura Secord 2. Jacques Cartier 3. Sir John A. Macdonald 4. Joseph Brant 5. Leif Eriksson
6. James Wolfe 7. Louis-Joseph de Montcalm 8. Harriet Tubman 9. Samuel de Champlain 10. Nellie McClung

Word Search *(page 92)*

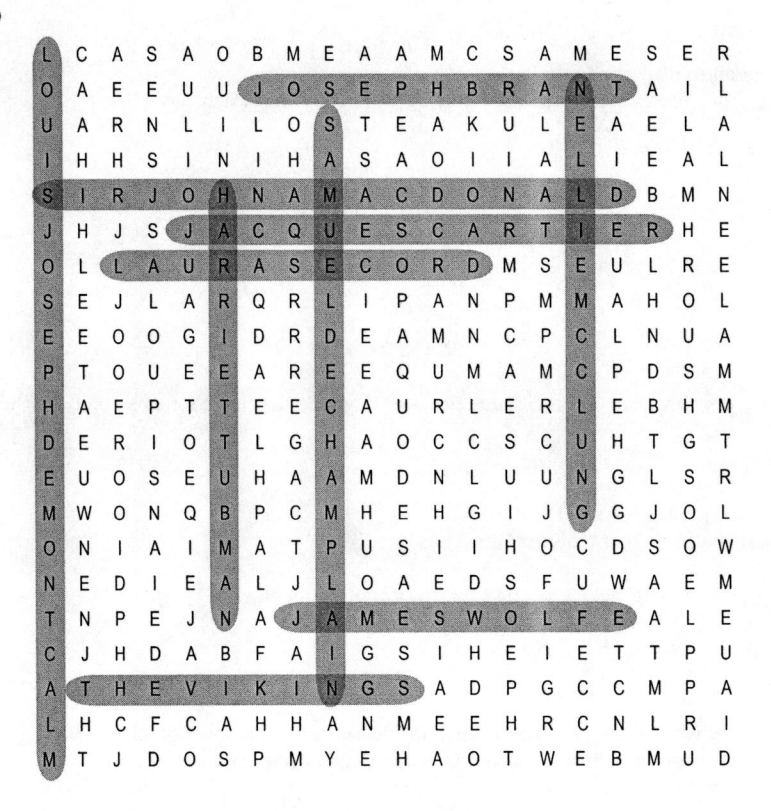

Crossword Puzzle *(page 93)*

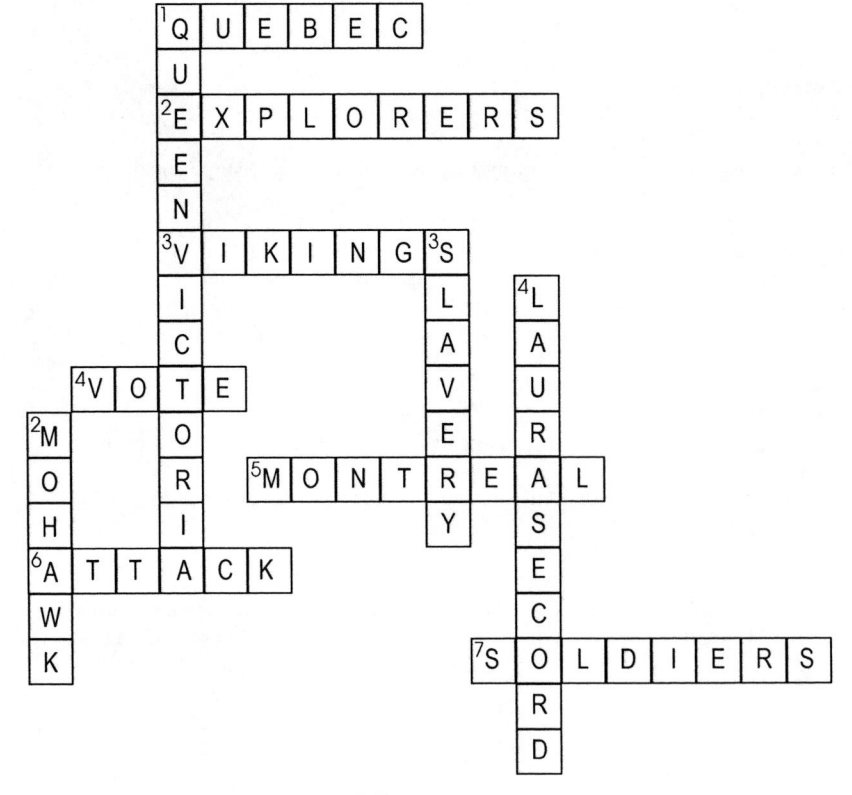

Publication Listing

See Dealer or www.sslearning.com For Pricing 1-800-463-6367

Code #	Title and Grade
SSC1-12	A Time of Plenty Gr. 2
SSN1-92	Abel's Island NS Gr. 4-6
SSF1-16	Aboriginal Peoples of Canada Gr. 7-8
SSK1-31	Addition & Subtraction Drills Gr. 1-3
SSK1-28	Addition Drills Gr. 1-3
SSY1-04	Addition Gr. 1-3
SSN1-174	Adv. of Huckle Berry Finn NS Gr. 7-8
SSB1-63	African Animals Gr 4-6
SSN1-267	Al Capone Does My Shirts NS Gr. 4-6
SSB1-29	All About Bears Gr. 1-2
SSF1-08	All About Boats Gr. 2-3
SSJ1-02	All About Canada Gr. 2
SSB1-54	All About Cattle Gr. 4-6
SSN1-10	All About Colours Gr. P-1
SSB1-93	All About Dinosaurs Gr. 2
SSN1-14	All About Dragons Gr. 3-5
SSB1-07	All About Elephants Gr. 3-4
SSB1-68	All About Fish Gr. 4-6
SSN1-39	All About Giants Gr. 2-3
SSH1-15	All About Jobs Gr. 1-3
SSH1-05	All About Me Gr. 1
SSA1-02	All About Mexico Gr. 4-6
SSR1-28	All About Nouns Gr. 5-7
SSF1-09	All About Planes Gr. 2-3
SSB1-33	All About Plants Gr. 2-3
SSR1-29	All About Pronouns Gr. 5-7
SSB1-12	All About Rabbits Gr. 2-3
SSB1-58	All About Spiders Gr. 4-6
SSA1-03	All About the Desert Gr. 4-6
SSA1-04	All About the Ocean Gr. 5-7
SSZ1-01	All About the Olympics Gr. 2-4
SSB1-49	All About the Sea Gr. 4-6
SSK1-06	All About Time Gr. 4-6
SSF1-07	All About Trains Gr. 2-3
SSH1-18	All About Transportation Gr. 2
SSB1-01	All About Trees Gr. 4-6
SSB1-61	All About Weather Gr. 7-8
SSB1-06	All About Whales Gr. 3-4
SSPC-26	All Kinds of Clocks B/W Pictures
SSB1-110	All Kinds of Structures Gr. 1
SSH1-19	All Kinds of Vehicles Gr. 3
SSF1-01	Amazing Aztecs Gr. 4-6
SSB1-92	Amazing Earthworms Gr. 2-3
SSJ1-50	Amazing Facts in Cdn History Gr. 4-6
SSB1-32	Amazing Insects Gr. 4-6
SSN1-132	Amelia Bedelia–Camping NS 1-3
SSN1-68	Amelia Bedelia NS 1-3
SSN1-155	Amelia Bedelia-Surprise Shower NS 1-3
SSA1-13	America The Beautiful Gr. 4-6
SSN1-57	Amish Adventure NS 7-8
SSF1-02	Ancient China Gr. 4-6
SSF1-18	Ancient Egypt Gr. 4-6
SSF1-21	Ancient Greece Gr. 4-6
SSF1-19	Ancient Rome Gr. 4-6
SSQ1-06	Animal Town – Big Book Pkg 1-3
SSQ1-02	Animals Prepare Winter – Big Book Pkg 1-3
SSN1-150	Animorphs the Invasion NS 4-6
SSN1-53	Anne of Green Gables NS 7-8
SSB1-40	Apple Celebration Gr. 4-6
SSB1-04	Apple Mania Gr. 2-3
SSB1-38	Apples are the Greatest Gr. P-K
SSB1-59	Arctic Animals Gr. 4-6
SSN1-162	Arnold Lobel Author Study Gr. 2-3
SSPC-22	Australia B/W Pictures
SSA1-05	Australia Gr. 5-8
SSM1-03	Autumn in the Woodlot Gr. 2-3
SSM1-08	Autumn Wonders Gr. 1
SSN1-41	Baby Sister for Frances NS 1-3
SSPC-19	Back to School B/W Pictures
SSC1-33	Back to School Gr. 2-3
SSN1-224	Banner in the Sky NS 7-8
SSN1-36	Bargain for Frances NS 1-3
SSB1-82	Bats Gr. 4-6
SSN1-71	BB – Drug Free Zone NS Gr. 1-3
SSN1-88	BB – In the Freaky House NS 1-3
SSN1-78	BB – Media Madness NS 1-3
SSN1-69	BB – Wheelchair Commando NS 1-3
SSN1-119	Be a Perfect Person-3 Days NS 4-6
SSC1-15	Be My Valentine Gr. 1

Code #	Title and Grade
SSD1-01	Be Safe Not Sorry Gr. P-1
SSN1-09	Bear Tales Gr. 2-4
SSB1-28	Bears Gr. 4-6
SSN1-202	Bears in Literature Gr. 1-3
SSN1-40	Beatrix Potter Gr. 2-4
SSN1-129	Beatrix Potter: Activity Biography Gr. 2-4
SSB1-47	Beautiful Bugs Gr. 1
SSB1-21	Beavers Gr. 3-5
SSN1-257	Because of Winn-Dixie NS Gr. 4-6
SSK1-04	Beginning Math Series: Calendar Gr. 2-3
SSR1-54	Beginning Cursive D. Gr. 2-4
SSR1-79	Beginning Cursive Z.B. Gr. 2-4
SSR1-53	Beginning Manuscript D. Gr. Pk-2
SSR1-76	Beginning Manuscript Z.B. Gr. PK-2
SSK1-08	Beginning Math Series: Shapes Gr. 1-3
SSK1-09	Beginning Math Series: Money CDN Gr. 1-3
SSK1-10	Beginning Math Series: Time Gr. 1-3
SSK1-22	Beginning Math Series: Measurement Gr. 1-3
SSK1-23	Beginning Math Series: Numbers Gr. 1-3
SSR1-58	Beginning and Practice Cursive D. Gr. 2-4
SSR1-82	Beginning and Practice Cursive Z.B. Gr. 2-4
SSR1-57	Beginning and Practice Manuscript D. Gr. PK-2
SSR1-83	Beginning and Practice Manuscript Z.B. Gr. Pk-2
SSN1-33	Bedtime for Frances NS 1-3
SSN1-114	Best Christmas Pageant Ever NS Gr. 4-6
SSN1-32	Best Friends for Frances NS Gr. 1-3
SSB1-39	Best Friends Pets Gr. P-K
SSN1-185	BFG NS Gr. 4-6
SSJ1-61	Big Book of Canadian Celebrations Gr. 1-3
SSJ1-62	Big Book of Canadian Celebrations Gr. 4-6
SSN1-35	Birthday for Frances NS Gr. 1-3
SSN1-107	Borrowers NS Gr. 4-6
SSC1-16	Bouquet of Valentines Gr. 2
SSN1-29	Bread & Jam for Frances NS Gr. 1-3
SSN1-63	Bridge to Terabithia NS Gr. 4-6
SSY1-24	BTS Numeración/Numeration Gr. 1-3
SSY1-25	BTS Adición/Addition Gr. 1-3
SSY1-26	BTS Sustracción/Subtraction Gr. 1-3
SSY1-27	BTS Fonética/Phonics Gr. 1-3
SSY1-28	BTS Leer para Entender/Reading for Understanding Gr. 1-3
SSY1-29	BTS Uso de las Mayúsculas y Reglas de Puntuación/Capitalization and Punctuation Gr. 1-3
SSY1-30	BTS Composición de Oraciones/ Sentence Writing Gr. 1-3
SSY1-31	BTS Composici13n de Historias/ Story Writing Gr. 1-3
SSN1-256	Bud, Not Buddy NS Gr. 4-6
SSB1-31	Bugs, Bugs & More Bugs Gr. 2-3
SSR1-07	Building Word Families L.V. Gr. 1-2
SSR1-05	Building Word Families S.V. Gr. 1-2
SSN1-204	Bunnicula NS Gr. 4-6
SSB1-80	Butterflies & Caterpillars Gr. 1-2
SSN1-164	Call It Courage NS Gr. 7-8
SSN1-67	Call of the Wild NS Gr. 7-8
SSJ1-41	Canada & It's Trading Partners 6-8
SSPC-28	Canada B/W Pictures
SSN1-173	Canada Geese Quilt NS Gr. 4-6
SSJ1-01	Canada Gr. 1
SSJ1-33	Canada's Capital Cities Gr. 4-6
SSJ1-43	Canada's Confederation Gr. 7-8
SSF1-04	Canada's First Nations Gr. 7-8
SSJ1-51	Canada's Landmarks Gr. 1-3
SSJ1-48	Canada's Landmarks Gr. 4-6
SSJ1-60	Canada's Links to the World Gr. 5-8
SSJ1-42	Canada's Traditions & Celeb. Gr. 1-3
SSB1-45	Canadian Animals Gr. 1-2
SSJ1-37	Canadian Arctic Inuit Gr. 2-3
SSJ1-53	Canadian Black History Gr. 4-8
SSJ1-57	Canadian Comprehension Gr. 1-2
SSJ1-58	Canadian Comprehension Gr. 3-4
SSJ1-59	Canadian Comprehension Gr. 5-6
SSJ1-46	Canadian Industries Gr. 4-6
SSK1-12	Canadian Problem Solving Gr. 4-6
SSJ1-38	Canadian Provinces & Terr. Gr. 4-6
SSY1-07	Capitalization & Punctuation Gr. 1-3
SSN1-198	Captain Courageous NS Gr. 7-8

Code #	Title and Grade
SSK1-11	Cars Problem Solving Gr. 3-4
R1-84	Cartoon Story Starters Gr. 1-3
R1-85	Cartoon Story Starters Gr. 4-6
SSN1-154	Castle in the Attic NS Gr. 4-6
SSF1-31	Castles & Kings Gr. 4-6
SSN1-144	Cat Ate My Gymsuit NS Gr. 4-6
SSPC-38	Cats B/W Pictures
SSB1-50	Cats – Domestic & Wild Gr. 4-6
SSN1-34	Cats in Literature Gr. 3-6
SSN1-212	Cay NS Gr. 7-8
SSM1-09	Celebrate Autumn Gr. 4-6
SSC1-39	Celebrate Christmas Gr. 4-6
SSC1-31	Celebrate Easter Gr. 4-6
SSC1-23	Celebrate Shamrock Day Gr. 2
SSM1-11	Celebrate Spring Gr. 4-6
SSC1-13	Celebrate Thanksgiving R. 3-4
SSM1-06	Celebrate Winter Gr. 4-6
SSB1-107	Cells, Tissues & Organs Gr. 7-8
SSB1-101	Characteristics of Flight Gr. 4-6
SSN1-66	Charlie & Chocolate Factory NS Gr. 4-6
SSN1-23	Charlotte's Web NS Gr. 4-6
SSB1-37	Chicks N'Ducks Gr. 2-4
SSA1-09	China Today Gr. 5-8
SSN1-70	Chocolate Fever NS Gr. 4-6
SSN1-241	Chocolate Touch NS Gr. 4-6
SSC1-38	Christmas Around the World Gr. 4-6
SSPC-42	Christmas B/W Pictures
SST1-08A	Christmas Gr. JK/SK
SST1-08B	Christmas Gr. 1
SST1-08C	Christmas Gr. 2-3
SSC1-04	Christmas Magic Gr. 1
SSC1-03	Christmas Tales Gr. 2-3
SSG1-06	Cinematography Gr. 5-8
SSPC-13	Circus B/W Pictures
SSF1-03	Circus Magic Gr. 3-4
SSJ1-52	Citizenship/Immigration Gr. 4-8
SSN1-104	Classical Poetry Gr. 7-12
SSN1-227	Color Gr. 1-3
SSN1-203	Colour Gr. 1-3
SSN1-135	Come Back Amelia Bedelia NS 1-3
SSH1-11	Community Helpers Gr. 1-3
SSK1-02	Concept Cards & Activities Gr. P-1
SSN1-183	Copper Sunrise NS Gr. 7-8
SSN1-86	Corduroy & Pocket Corduroy NS 1-3
SSN1-124	Could Dracula Live in Wood NS 4-6
SSN1-148	Cowboy's Don't Cry NS Gr. 7-8
SSR1-01	Creativity with Food Gr. 4-8
SSB1-34	Creatures of the Sea Gr. 2-4
SSN1-208	Curse of the Viking Grave NS 7-8
SSN1-134	Danny Champion of World NS 4-6
SSN1-98	Danny's Run NS Gr. 7-8
SSK1-21	Data Management Gr. 4-6
SSB1-53	Dealing with Dinosaurs Gr. 4-6
SSN1-178	Dear Mr. Henshaw NS Gr. 4-6
SSB1-22	Deer Gr. 3-5
SSPC-20	Desert B/W Pictures
SSJ1-40	Development of Western Canada 7-8
SSA1-16	Development of Manufacturing 7-9
SSN1-105	Dicken's Christmas NS Gr. 7-8
SSN1-62	Different Dragons NS Gr. 4-6
SSPC-21	Dinosaurs B/W Pictures
SSB1-16	Dinosaurs Gr. 1
SSB1-98	Dinosaurs Gr. 3
SST1-02A	Dinosaurs Gr. JK/SK
SST1-02B	Dinosaurs Gr. 1
SST1-02 C	Dinosaurs Gr. 2-3
SSN1-175	Dinosaurs in Literature Gr. 1-3
SSJ1-26	Discover Nova Scotia Gr. 5-7
SSJ1-36	Discover Nunavut Territory Gr. 5-7
SSJ1-25	Discover Ontario Gr. 5-7
SSJ1-24	Discover PEI Gr. 5-7
SSJ1-22	Discover Québec Gr. 5-7
SSL1-01	Discovering the Library Gr. 2-3
SSB1-106	Diversity of Living Things Gr. 4-6
SSK1-27	Division Drills Gr. 4-6
SSB1-30	Dogs – Wild & Tame Gr. 4-6
SSPC-31	Dogs B/W Pictures
SSN1-196	Dog's Don't Tell Jokes NS Gr. 4-6
SSN1-182	Door in the Wall NS Gr. 4-6
SSB1-87	Down by the Sea Gr. 1-3
SSN1-189	Dr. Jeckyll & Mr. Hyde NS Gr. 4-6
SSG1-07	Dragon Trivia Gr. P-8
SSN1-102	Dragon's Egg NS Gr. 4-6
SSN1-16	Dragons in Literature Gr. 3-6
SSC1-06	Early Christmas Gr. 3-5
SSB1-109	Earth's Crust Gr. 6-8
SSC1-21	Easter Adventures Gr. 3-4
SSC1-17	Easter Delights Gr. P-K
SSC1-19	Easter Surprises Gr. 1
SSPC-12	Egypt B/W Pictures
SSN1-255	Egypt Game NS Gr. 4-6

Code #	Title and Grade
SSF1-28	Egyptians Today & Yesterday Gr. 2-3
SSJ1-49	Elections in Canada Gr. 4-8
SSB1-108	Electricity Gr. 4-6
SSN1-02	Elves & the Shoemaker NS Gr. 1-3
SSH1-14	Emotions Gr. P-2
SSB1-85	Energy Gr. 4-6
SSN1-108	English Language Gr. 10-12
SSN1-156	Enjoying Eric Wilson Series Gr. 5-7
SSB1-64	Environment Gr. 4-6
SSR1-12	ESL Teaching Ideas Gr. K-8
SSN1-258	Esperanza Rising NS Gr. 4-6
SSR1-22	Exercises in Grammar Gr. 6
SSR1-23	Exercises in Grammar Gr. 7
SSR1-24	Exercises in Grammar Gr. 8
SSF1-20	Exploration Gr. 4-6
SSF1-15	Explorers & Mapmakers of Can. 7-8
SSJ1-54	Exploring Canada Gr. 1-3
SSJ1-56	Exploring Canada Gr. 1-6
SSJ1-55	Exploring Canada Gr. 4-6
SSH1-20	Exploring My School & Community 1
SSPC-39	Fables B/W Pictures
SSN1-15	Fables Gr. 4-6
SSN1-04	Fairy Tale Magic Gr. 3-5
SSPC-11	Fairy Tales B/W Pictures
SSN1-11	Fairy Tales Gr. 1-2
SSN1-199	Family Under the Bridge NS Gr. 4-6
SSPC-41	Famous Canadians B/W Pictures
SSJ1-12	Famous Canadians Gr. 4-8
SSN1-210	Fantastic Mr. Fox NS Gr. 4-6
SSB1-36	Fantastic Plants Gr. 4-6
SSPC-04	Farm Animals B/W Pictures
SSB1-15	Farm Animals Gr. 1-2
SST1-03A	Farm Gr. JK/SK
SST1-03B	Farm Gr. 1
SST1-03C	Farm Gr. 2-3
SSJ1-05	Farming Community Gr. 3-4
SSB1-44	Farmyard Friends Gr. P-K
SSJ1-45	Fathers of Confederation Gr. 4-8
SSB1-19	Feathered Friends Gr. 4-6
SST1-05A	February Gr. JK/SK
SST1-05B	February Gr. 1
SST1-05C	February Gr. 2-3
SSN1-03	Festival of Fairytales Gr. 3-5
SSC1-36	Festivals Around the World Gr. 2-3
SSN1-168	First 100 Sight Words Gr. 1
SSC1-32	First Days at School Gr. 1
SSJ1-06	Fishing Community Gr. 3-4
SSN1-170	Flowers for Algernon NS Gr. 7-8
SSN1-261	Flat Stanley NS Gr. 1-3
SSN1-128	Fly Away Home NS Gr. 4-6
SSD1-05	Food: Fact, Fun & Fiction Gr. 1-3
SSD1-06	Food: Nutrition & Invention Gr. 4-6
SSB1-118	Force and Motion Gr. 1-3
SSB1-119	Force and Motion Gr. 4-6
SSB1-25	Foxes Gr. 3-5
SSN1-263	Fractured Fairy Tales NS Gr. 1-3
SSN1-172	Freckle Juice NS Gr. 1-3
SSB1-43	Friendly Frogs Gr. 1
SSN1-260	Frindle NS Gr. 4-6
SSB1-89	Fruits & Seeds Gr. 4-6
SSN1-137	Fudge-a-Mania NS Gr. 4-6
SSB1-14	Fun on the Farm Gr. 3-4
SSR1-49	Fun with Phonics Gr. 1-3
SSPC-06	Garden Flowers B/W Pictures
SSK1-03	Geometric Shapes Gr. 2-5
SSC1-18	Get the Rabbit Habit Gr. 1-2
SSN1-209	Giver, The NS Gr. 7-8
SSN1-190	Go Jump in the Pool NS Gr. 4-6
SSG1-03	Goal Setting Gr. 6-8
SSG1-08	Gr. 3 Test – Parent Guide
SSG1-99	Gr. 3 Test – Teacher Guide
SSG1-09	Gr. 6 Language Test–Parent Guide
SSG1-97	Gr. 6 Language Test–Teacher Guide
SSG1-10	Gr. 6 Math Test – Parent Guide
SSG1-96	Gr. 6 Math Test – Teacher Guide
SSG1-98	Gr. 6 Math/Lang. Test–Teacher Guide
SSK1-14	Graph for all Seasons Gr. 1-3
SSN1-117	Great Brain NS Gr. 4-6
SSN1-90	Great Expectations NS Gr. 7-8
SSN1-169	Great Gilly Hopkins NS Gr. 4-6
SSN1-197	Great Science Fair Disaster NS Gr. 4-6
SSN1-138	Greek Mythology Gr. 7-8
SSN1-113	Green Gables Detectives NS 4-6
SSC1-26	Groundhog Celebration Gr. 2
SSC1-25	Groundhog Day Gr. 1
SSB1-113	Growth & Change in Animals Gr. 2-3
SSB1-114	Growth & Change in Plants Gr. 2-3
SSB1-48	Guinea Pigs & Friends Gr. 3-5
SSB1-104	Habitats Gr. 4-6
SSPC-18	Halloween B/W Pictures
SST1-04A	Halloween Gr. JK/SK

Publication Listing

Publication Listing

Code #	Title and Grade
SST1-09C	Thanksgiving Gr. 2-3
SSN1-77	There's a Boy in the Girls... NS 4-6
SSN1-143	This Can't Be Happening NS 4-6
SSN1-05	Three Billy Goats Gruff NS Gr. 1-3
SSN1-72	Ticket to Curlew NS Gr. 4-6
SSN1-82	Timothy of the Cay NS Gr. 7-8
SSF1-32	Titanic Gr. 4-6
SSN1-222	To Kill a Mockingbird NS Gr. 7-8
SSN1-195	Toilet Paper Tigers NS Gr. 4-6
SSJ1-35	Toronto Gr. 4-8
SSH1-02	Toy Shelf Gr. P-K
SSPC-24	Toys B/W Pictures
SSN1-163	Traditional Poetry Gr. 7-10
SSH1-13	Transportation Gr. 4-6
SSW1-01	Transportation Snip Art
SSB1-03	Trees Gr. 2-3
SSA1-01	Tropical Rainforest Gr. 4-6
SSN1-56	Trumpet of the Swan NS Gr. 4-6
SSN1-81	Tuck Everlasting NS Gr. 4-6
SSN1-126	Turtles in Literature Gr. 1-3
SSN1-270	Underground to Canada NS 4-6
SSN1-27	Unicorns in Literature Gr. 3-5
SSJ1-44	Upper & Lower Canada Gr. 7-8
SSN1-192	Using Novels Canadian North Gr. 7-8
SSC1-14	Valentines Day Gr. 5-8
SSPC-45	Vegetables B/W Pictures
SSY1-01	Very Hungry Caterpillar NS 30/Pkg Gr. 1-3
SSF1-13	Victorian Era Gr. 7-8
SSC1-35	Victorian Christmas Gr. 5-8
SSF1-17	Viking Age Gr. 4-6
SSN1-206	War with Grandpa SN Gr. 4-6
SSB1-91	Water Gr. 2-4
SSN1-166	Watership Down NS Gr. 7-8
SSH1-16	Ways We Travel Gr. P-K
SSN1-101	Wayside Sch. Little Stranger NS Gr. 4-6
SSN1-76	Wayside Sch. is Falling Down NS 4-6
SSB1-60	Weather Gr. 4-6
SSN1-17	Wee Folk in Literature Gr. 3-5
SSPC-08	Weeds B/W Pictures
SSQ1-04	Welcome Back – Big Book Pkg 1-3
SSB1-73	Whale Preservation Gr. 5-8
SSH1-08	What is a Community? Gr. 2-4
SSH1-01	What is a Family? Gr. 2-3
SSH1-09	What is a School? Gr. 1-2
SSJ1-32	What is Canada? Gr. P-K
SSN1-79	What is RAD? Read & Discover 2-4
SSB1-62	What is the Weather Today? Gr. 2-4
SSN1-194	What's a Daring Detective NS 4-6
SSH1-10	What's My Number Gr. P-K
SSR1-02	What's the Scoop on Words Gr. 4-6
SSN1-73	Where the Red Fern Grows NS Gr. 7-8
SSN1-87	Where the Wild Things Are NS Gr. 1-3
SSN1-187	Whipping Boy NS Gr. 4-6
SSN1-226	Who is Frances Rain? NS Gr. 4-6
SSN1-74	Who's Got Gertie & How...? NS Gr. 4-6
SSN1-131	Why did the Underwear ... NS 4-6
SSC1-28	Why Wear a Poppy? Gr. 2-3
SSJ1-11	Wild Animals of Canada Gr. 2-3
SSPC-07	Wild Flowers B/W Pictures
SSB1-18	Winter Birds Gr. 2-3
SSZ1-03	Winter Olympics Gr. 4-6
SSM1-04	Winter Wonderland Gr. 1
SSC1-01	Witches Gr. 3-4
SSN1-213	Wolf Island NS Gr. 1-3
SSE1-09	Wolfgang Amadeus Mozart 6-9
SSB1-23	Wolves Gr. 3-5
SSC1-20	Wonders of Easter Gr. 2
SSY1-15	Word Families Gr. 1-3
SSR1-59	Word Families 2,3 Letter Words Gr. 1-3
SSR1-60	Word Families 3, 4 Letter Words Gr. 1-3
SSR1-61	Word Families 2, 3, 4 Letter Words Big Book Gr. 1-3
SSB1-35	World of Horses Gr. 4-6
SSB1-13	World of Pets Gr. 2-3
SSF1-26	World War II Gr. 7-8
SSN1-221	Wrinkle in Time NS Gr. 7-8
SSPC-02	Zoo Animals B/W Pictures
SSB1-08	Zoo Animals Gr. 1-2
SSB1-09	Zoo Celebration Gr. 3-4